COMMUNITY PARTNER GUIDE TO CAMPUS COLLABORATIONS

COMMUNITY PARTNER GUIDE TO CAMPUS COLLABORATIONS

Enhance Your Community by Becoming a Co-Educator With Colleges and Universities

Christine M. Cress, Stephanie T. Stokamer, and

Joyce P. Kaufman

STERLING, VIRGINIA

COPYRIGHT © 2015 BY
STYLUS PUBLISHING, LLC

Published by Stylus Publishing, LLC
22883 Quicksilver Drive
Sterling, Virginia 20166-2102

Library of Congress Cataloging-in-Publication Data
Cress, Christine M. (Christine Marie), 1962
Community partner guide to campus collaborations : enhance your community by becoming a co-educator with colleges and universities / Christine M. Cress, Stephanie T. Stokamer, and Joyce P. Kaufman.
  pages cm
Includes bibliographical references and index.
ISBN 978-1-62036-136-8 (pbk. : alk. paper)
ISBN 978-1-62036-135-1 (cloth : alk. paper)
ISBN 978-1-62036-137-5 (library networkable e-edition)
ISBN 978-1-62036-138-2 (consumer e-edition)
1. Community and college. 2. Service learning. I. Stokamer, Stephanie Taylor. II. Title.
LC237.C74 2015
372.42'5–dc23

2014034237

13-digit ISBN: 978-1-62036-135-1 (cloth)
13-digit ISBN: 978-1-62036-136-8 (paperback)
13-digit ISBN: 978-1-62036-137-5 (library networkable e-edition)
13-digit ISBN: 978-1-62036-138-2 (consumer e-edition)

The paperback edition is also available in sets of 6 or 12, at reduced prices, to facilitate its use for planning, and for training of leaders engaged in partnerships. Visit www.Styluspub.com or call 1-800-232-0223 to order.
13-digit ISBN: 978-1-62036-271-6 (set of 6)
978-1-62036-272-3 (set of 12)

Printed in the United States of America

All first editions printed on acid-free paper
that meets the American National Standards Institute
Z39-48 Standard.

Bulk Purchases

Quantity discounts are available for use in workshops
and for staff development.
Call 1-800-232-0223

First Edition, 2015

10   9   8   7   6   5   4   3   2   1

For Beau, Suraj, and AJ
Future change agents of enriching communities

CONTENTS

INTRODUCTION

The Possibilities and Pitfalls of Campus-Community Partnerships

Overview: This chapter highlights the challenges and potential of community-campus relationships through various forms of civic engagement including myriad opportunities that exist for making real community impact and supporting student learning and growth. Community partners are encouraged to initiate mutually enriching collaborations with colleges and are offered a five-step framework for *exploring, establishing, engaging, empowering,* and *evaluating* effective and enriching community-campus collaborations.

- Considerations for Connecting With Colleges
- Clarifying Confusing Terminology
- Creating Enriching Collaborations for Community Enhancement

Considerations for Connecting With Colleges

Across the United States and around the world, when community agencies partner with colleges, the outcomes can be powerful and full of possibilities. For example, students not only can learn the roots of poverty but through serving also come to understand that the materialistically poor have capacity, voice, and dignity that can help leverage individual and community change. In turn, clients who might have lost hope may find new energy and resources offered by the fresh perspectives of college students. **When communities and colleges collaborate, their collective impact can be greater than their individual efforts.**

The Reverend Martin Luther King Jr. understood the potential power of collaborations when he stated that *everyone can be great because everyone can serve* (Holloran & Carson, 2000). In the spirit of courage and possibility, Dr. King sought to forge common ground on which people from all walks of life could join together as equals to address important community issues. And service, he realized, was the great equalizer (Corporation for National and Community Service, 2005).

To that end, joint college and community agency relationships that include forms of volunteerism, community service, and civic engagement have been on the rise the past two decades as a means to advance student learning and community improvement. In the Americas, Asia, Europe, Africa, India, and Australia, college students and faculty are increasingly seeking community-based learning opportunities to make sense of abstract concepts in context and make meaningful change through the application of ideas, knowledge, and skills. As well, professionals in the community have realized that tapping the resources of colleges can have an exponential effect on their ability to address community needs and create systemic improvement.

As such, if you are at a nonprofit organization, you may already have years of experience working with university interns or volunteers, but you might be looking for deeper insights and proven strategies for increasing the efficiency and effectiveness of your organization. Alternatively, you may be new to your position within a city, state, or national agency and wondering how you might utilize the resources of your local college to improve client services and encourage student learning about community needs and assets. Or you may represent a nongovernmental organization (NGO) interested in partnering with colleges on different continents in order to leverage community improvement and bring attention to the challenges, resources, and needs of your population.

Thus, whether you are a seasoned expert or a relative novice in connecting with higher education institutions, this *Community Partner Guide* and the tips and techniques included here are designed to leverage *learning* and *community empowerment* for both clients and colleges. (In using the term *colleges*, we intend this to be inclusive of technical or vocational schools above the high school level, community colleges, 4-year colleges, and universities.)

Depending on the country, many community agency coordinators and NGO directors may have attended college and therefore have some understanding of higher education. For example, Mexico has a mandatory service component for all students enrolled in higher education, and forms of college-level community-based service are becoming increasingly required in North America, Europe, Asia, and Australia.

Therefore, as a community agency representative, you may have as a college student volunteered at a neighborhood association that piqued your own academic and career interests in community and social services. Or maybe you had a chance to partake in a college service day at the food bank or participate in an alternative spring break trip that constructed homes for those affected by a natural disaster. Maybe, even, you had a faculty member or instructor who connected community service experiences with course content.

Of course, regardless of your own educational background, there are also many K–12 school administrators and teachers reaching out to community organizations to form partnerships for education and community engagement. Indeed, you or your agency may already be collaborating with high school or middle school students to assist with community programming or client services. In fact, there is a long and proven track record of community agency and campus collaborations that have included a third partnership with K–12 public schools, teachers, and districts, as well as with private, religious-affiliated, and charter schools.

When well-designed and thoughtfully conducted collaborations occur between community professionals and college faculty and administrators, community needs are addressed, and college students' personal and professional development is facilitated. Various types of volunteering, community service, and service-learning (more on these definitions later in the chapter) have been shown to increase high school graduation rates of at-risk youth, promote enrollment in higher education degree programs, decrease juvenile recidivism, and increase the economic stability of neighborhoods, to name just a few outcomes. Community-campus collaborations improve our educational, social, environmental, health, and business assets on the individual and organizational levels. Thus, both the community and the campus are *mutually* and *reciprocally enhanced* by such connections.

In essence, the possibilities of community-campus collaborations are endless. But so, too, can be the pitfalls. Even the most well-intentioned community agency professionals and their academic colleagues can encounter multiple unanticipated problems. As well, you may find that traversing the landscape of academe and higher education institutions (as compared to a high school or school district) can be a frustrating and daunting task in your role as a community service organizer. For example, students may arrive at your organization unannounced and with little to no understanding of the services you offer the community but insist that they "must provide 10 hours of service" to meet their course requirement. Or a faculty member may call to coordinate a collaborative research project with your agency, which you spend time planning, and then the instructor and students never show. Or the tasks that you need for service-learning students to complete are not what they expected (such as making copies and sharpening pencils before they assist high school students with homework), and they don't do them. Or they perform such tasks but only reluctantly and with poor attitudes that undermine the value of the work and the clients you are serving.

Unreturned e-mail and vague phone messages from students and faculty have resulted in community representatives feeling frustrated, let down, confused, resentful, inconvenienced, burdened, and disappointed (real terms used by actual agency directors).

Pitfalls:

- Students who don't show up
- Students who have no understanding of your organization or clients
- Students who show up in midriffs, short shorts, and flip-flops and want to save the world
- Faculty who don't return phone calls or e-mail
- Faculty who accompany students to the service site and try to run the show
- A lack of understanding of client and community issues
- Inappropriate and ignorant remarks and behavior

Indeed, expectations for roles, tasks, training, supervision, and evaluation can be fraught with miscommunication and misunderstanding. And the issues can range from being merely laughable, such as when college students wore flimsy sandals to lead fifth graders on a 3-mile nature hike, to highly liable, such as when college students gave car rides home to the fifth graders.

So why consider connecting to colleges, sometimes referred to as the "ivory tower"? Given the potential for uninformed and elitist attitudes that can be expressed by faculty and students and the sheer effort and energy it can take to organize such collaborations, *why do it*?

Quite frankly, some community organizations simply have no choice. They may need the volunteer bodies from colleges to meet their service and client goals. Others may also depend on the future philanthropy of alumni volunteers to buoy their meager operating budgets.

But there are also deeper and more meaningful reasons for initiating and investing in community-campus collaborations. In short, **effective community-campus relationships educate students and enhance communities**. In fact, there is a rich history of colleges and communities conjoining for common purposes. For instance, Jane Addams at the turn of the twentieth century involved university students at Hull House, which influenced the academic fields of sociology and social services. John Dewey, a faculty member at the University of Chicago, proved that community-based learning and reflection was a more effective educational method than mere reading and lecture.

More recently, a group of college presidents formed Campus Compact, a national organization that is dedicated to facilitating collaborations between communities and colleges for the purposes of promoting effective learning and serving. Specifically, Campus Compact funds and manages directors in over 30 U.S. states whose explicit charge is to link college campuses with community organizations in order to bolster the educational and economic resources of cities and the nation (see www.compact.org).

Such sentiments are shared by U.S. president Barack Obama, who, in a commencement address to the Ohio State University graduating class of 2013, compelled students to find not just a career but a cause for the greater good and aspire to be citizens who value both individual rights and community responsibilities (Calmes, 2013).

Similarly, Portland State University president Wim Wiewel (2010) asserted that connecting the institutional missions and educational goals of colleges with those of community organizations through thoughtfully designed civic engagement experiences improves student learning outcomes and strengthens the educational, economic, and social assets of colleges and communities alike.

Importantly, research bears out these claims. The National Conference on Citizenship (2011) highlighted data findings that civic engagement strengthens the economy through positive neighborhood interactions that garner community problem solving, small business investment, and consumer spending (see also Kawashima-Ginsberg, Lim, & Levine, 2012).

In addition, California Campus Compact reported that campus-community partnerships through service-learning and civic engagement foster economic, educational, and social vitality through microfinance and social entrepreneurship (Plaut,

Cress, Ikeda, & McGinley, 2013). Moreover, such partnerships had a significantly positive effect on the educational achievement and aspirations of first-generation and low-income students. In fact, one educator (Gent, 2007) claimed that collaborations between colleges and communities are one way to ensure that *no child is left behind*.

> **High School Student:** "Service-learning motivates me to keep going. I now see how education can benefit me and my community."

These statistics are evidenced in *A Promising Connection: Increasing College Access and Success Through Civic Engagement* (www.compact.org/resources-for-presidents). At both the K–12 and higher education levels, students who participate in service-learning and civic engagement experiences (as either facilitators or receivers of the service) are more likely to graduate from high school, attend college, and become future volunteers in their communities (Cress, Burack, Giles, Elkins, & Stevens, 2010).

Certainly, in addition to the benefits that K–12 and college students realize as a result of effective collaborations between community organizations and higher education institutions, the resources and reach of agencies are strengthened. The number of clients who can be assisted is increased, the number of agency staff who can expand the level of their professional activities is improved, the number and types of support services and programs can be extended, and the opportunities for human resource and fiscal stabilization are augmented.

> **Community Partner:** "The college students brought knowledge and skills to our clients and staff that we just don't have the resources to provide. They taught them computer skills, updated our website, and created an online tracking system for hits on our resources sites."

In sum, communities are stronger when campuses and community agencies collaborate because it creates knowledgeable and engaged students who give back to their communities as committed citizens long after they graduate.

Possibilities: Community agencies benefit from the following:

- Students who assist and inspire clients
- Students who demonstrate leadership and insight to improve services

- Faculty who communicate frequently and want to meet your goals
- Faculty who desire long-term and reciprocal partnerships
- Faculty who prepare students' knowledge, skills, and attitudes for learning and serving
- Staff who can extend their professional expertise to new areas and programs
- Clients who are better served
- Communities that are improved

> **College Student:** "I wouldn't be in college today if it hadn't been for service-learning in my high school. Students from Southern State helped me fill out the application and financial aid forms. No one in my family had been to college, so we had no idea what to do. At the Boys and Girls Club where I volunteer, I let the kids know that they should go to college."

Clarifying Confusing Terminology

We assume that to some extent you are already convinced of or likely to be converted to the concept of community-campus collaborations—otherwise, you would probably not be reviewing this community partner guide! In fact, it may be that a college colleague provided you with this resource guide or you received it when you attended a college orientation program for community agencies sponsored by your local college. As such, you may not need a plethora of statistics and data to prove the powerful learning and community impact potential of such partnerships. You have seen it, worked it, and lived it!

Use the appendix

Still, if you are writing a grant or completing a report for a stakeholder (such as a philanthropic donor or elected representative), being able to identify and cite research sources can be helpful in linking your efforts with those of others. This guide contains an appendix of resources, websites, professional associations, and journals that may be of assistance to you.

In fact, throughout the text you will see the strategy icon (⊕) to highlight strategies for navigating the academic fields of service-learning and community-based learning, as well as the landscapes of higher education campuses. Look for this quick reference symbol if you are quickly scanning the page for quick tips and tools.

Also, you may want to review a separate compendium of research data and statistics to get you started in understanding the lay of the land. *A Crucible Moment: College Learning and Democracy's Future* (see www.aacu.org/civic_learning/crucible) is a report from the National Task Force on Civic Learning and Democratic Engagement (2012) that calls on educators and community leaders to make civic learning and community engagement an expected part of every student's education.

Likewise, the International Association for Research on Service-Learning and Community Engagement (IARSLCE) includes 1,000 members from over 30 countries committed to researching and promoting best practices for improving learning and civic outcomes (see www.researchslce.org).

Around the world, administrators, researchers, and educators are looking for academic engagement paths to partner with community agencies and NGOs for the sake of learning and community improvement. This is an opportunity for you to join the conversation and vocalize your ideas about strategies for realizing mutual benefits.

Although we understand that your ultimate goal is to be a *co-agent* of community change and improvement, this concept and the terminology may be difficult to understand and embrace for many faculty and students. Alternatively, we suggest that you consider positioning yourself within the terrain of academe as a *co-educator*. We are not suggesting that the onus is fully on you to create the collaboration. Rather, we encourage you to move toward academe in ways that administrators, faculty, and students may more readily understand as they, in turn, try to adjust their frames of reference in moving toward you and the community. Thus, this Community Partner Guide is to help you navigate and map out how to become a co-educator in the empowerment, enhancement, and enrichment of students, colleges, and communities.

Understanding higher education jargon and terminology; making sense of various academic acronyms and symbols; and being able to "talk" the language with college administrators, students, or faculty can be critical in communicating your goals and expectations, because each form of collaboration varies. Therefore, whether you are doing an Internet search on outcomes-based research or you are writing an e-mail to a faculty member about a prospective service activity, you may find the following terms and standard definitions useful.

We begin by differentiating among the titles applied to individuals providing the service. Although community organizations or colleges may use these terms interchangeably, the underlying purposes and expectations are distinct.

- A *volunteer* is an unpaid (or uncompensated) individual providing service, doing tasks, or offering other forms of assistance. Their purpose is to help the organization or client.
- An *intern* may be a paid or unpaid individual performing tasks in expectation of learning new skills or knowledge for career enhancement. Student interns may (or may not) also get course credit for their work with a community-based organization.
- *Service-learners* are unpaid students from a college program or course who provide service while reflecting from an academic perspective on antecedents

and possible leverage points for individual, community, and systemic improvement. In short, service-learners are college students engaged in learning through serving.

- *Community partners* are representatives at the community organization or agency who facilitate the volunteer, intern, or service-learner experience.

We hope these titles are relatively clear. But when they are applied to differing agencies, colleges, and courses, the precise definitions of words and phrases can have alternate meanings and expectations, as activities (types of service) and reasons for those activities (knowledge or skill application) are associated with various organizational realms (see Figure 1.1).

Be clear about definitions

Unfortunately, at the conceptual and organizational levels, the terminology can become far more confusing, because agencies, colleges, and individual faculty may use different terms to mean the same thing (such as *community-based learning* and *service-learning*). Or the same term can mean different things (such as *civic engagement*). Usually, the distinctions are implicitly embedded with underlying expectations and purposes and therefore may take multiple conversations to clarify. For your purposes in becoming a co-educator, though, it is worth the time and effort to have these conversations so that everyone is clear about the definitions and the associated role and task expectations.

- *Civic engagement* is an umbrella term that is applied to multiple forms of engagement where students are interacting with and learning about the larger civic community, whether as a whole concept, such as democracy, or in part, such as registering individuals to vote. Colleges often use this term to connote collaborative relationships with communities, whether they involve volunteer, internship, or service-learning experiences.
- *Community service* is normally applied to volunteer service off campus (at a community agency) but may be used for service to the college community

Figure 1.1.   Community engagement and academic study interactions.

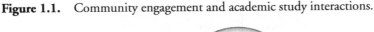

(such as picking up litter on a campus green space). This term is also used by the judicial court system in lieu of imprisonment. Rather than receiving jail time or a fine, an individual may be required to complete community service hours. Finally, faculty may use this term to refer to their own campus community service on committees or other college administrative tasks.

- *Community-based learning* is used by colleges to denote out-of-classroom, experiential, or problem-based learning that occurs in the community. Community-based learning may be performed by individual students or as a class project. It may include intentional civic and service components or reflections.
- Community or civic service that is integrated into course content, learning, engagement, and reflection is referred to as *service-learning*. Students provide direct service to clients (e.g., tutoring) or complete indirect service projects (e.g., updating an agency website) for community organizations in order to apply, reflect on, and evaluate the relevance of the disciplinary knowledge of their courses to community challenges.
- *Community-based research* is research and assessment that is conducted by students and faculty in conjunction with community partners.

Certainly, the subtleties and nuances of these terms can be perplexing. As noted previously, one college may use the term *community-based learning* for their courses, whereas another uses *service-learning*. Students may speak in terms of *community service*, whereas a college administrator may use the language of *civic engagement*.

At Spokane Falls Community College, *service-learning* is defined as follows:

Service-Learning is a method of teaching and learning that engages students in meaningful service to their community through careful integration of academic instruction. Service-Learning gives students an opportunity to use knowledge gained in the classroom to address needs in the neighborhood.

At Eastern Washington University, *service-learning* is defined in this way:

Service-Learning is the formal integration of meaningful community service with classroom instruction and reflection to enhance student learning, teach civic responsibility, and strengthen communities.

Similarly, the International Christian University in Tokyo, Japan, defines *service-learning* as follows:

Service-Learning is different from volunteer work. Generally speaking, service-learning is a way of putting education back into society, of linking what students learn in the classroom to what goes on in the real world; it is a way of encouraging students to be useful and productive in the service of others, and it provides students with means of developing skills related to interacting with others who are unlike themselves. It is a method of teaching, learning, and reflecting which builds academic instruction with practical service in community.

What you probably notice about each of these three examples is that *service-learning* is a hyphenated term and is explained as an explicit connection between academic learning and increased social awareness through community service experiences.

Therefore, rather than being frustrated by the inconsistencies, try to understand the motivations driving the collaborations. Ask for clarification by stating, "This is how I define 'service-learning.' . . . Does this have the same meaning for you?" Or consider showing Figure 1.1 to your college contact (e.g., administrator, student, or faculty) and inquire, "Where on the diagram do you imagine this campus-community collaboration?"

Often additional insights about definitions, principles, and values that might be driving college initiatives for collaborating with the community can be gleaned from surfing and carefully reviewing college, department, office, course, or faculty websites. For example, stated on the website—as well as displayed on the concrete pedestrian bridge—at Portland State University is the motto "Let Knowledge Serve the City."

Understand the motivations

At Whittier College, the institutional mission and framing purpose for its Center for Engagement With Communities (which includes facilitation of volunteering, service-learning, community-based learning, and community-based research) is to "equip Whittier students to be active citizens and effective communicators who embrace diversity and act with integrity by becoming actively involved in the local community as they explore their role in the global community."

Perhaps not surprising, at Holy Names University and the Center for Social Justice and Civic Engagement, their sponsorship of academic engagement with the community (in the form of internships, experiential learning, study abroad, and community-based learning) is rooted in traditions of their Catholic faith beliefs for empowering students for leadership and service in a diverse world.

Thus, whether for educational, philosophical, or religious reasons, discerning how campus-community collaboration fits with each organization's vision, mission, principles, and practices can help individuals identify common linkages for potential civic engagement connections.

Of course, in truth for most faculty and college administrators—even if they are from a religious institution with mission statements containing the words *service, justice,* or *charity*—connecting students with the community is not simply about "doing good." Colleges are educational institutions; they are not service organizations. As such, for colleges the concept of civic

"Sometimes we get calls from students stating that they need to 'fulfill their community service hour requirements.' Our first question is: 'Are you being sent by the judicial courts or a college faculty?' Clarifying 'service' roles and tasks is critical to maintaining effective client programs."

engagement is primarily about learning, not serving. Ideally, of course, the two goals and concepts reinforce one another.

Clearly, the differences in the basic operating premises between colleges and community agencies have left many community partners feeling used and exploited by students, faculty, and administrators. The result of these differences has led to reluctance and rejection by some community partners to accept college student volunteers, interns, and service-learners. On a grander scale, entire town-gown relationships have suffered and soured when the community has felt manipulated by the college. In one city, the college claimed to be the "flame of light and enlightenment," but in contrast the townspeople felt burned by the "hot egos" of faculty and students (a true story!).

Creating Enriching Collaborations for Community Enhancement

Thus, although college presidents may wax eloquently about *reciprocal* and *synergistic* community-campus relationships (more on these terms in chapters 2 and 3), the realities are that mutually beneficial and sustainable collaborations are built through the individual interactions and continued perseverance of community partners, students, and faculty.

To achieve reciprocity in such relationships, community partners must become co-educators in the educational engagement endeavor. Your community partner role contributes directly to students' education because you help students apply what they learn in the classroom. In turn, both the campus and the client community are enhanced and enriched.

> "Students participated in a variety of community-building activities from designing sustainable community gardens allowing low-income residents access to healthy food to facilitating intergenerational art events that encouraged new dialogues between neighbors."

- **But what might be some steps or strategies for achieving a co-educational role?**
- **And how can this be accomplished when disparities in power often exist between academic institutions and community agencies and the individuals within them?**

These were the questions asked of us in our collective experiences with scores of community professionals across North America. In turn, we asked community agency and NGO representatives, staff, and directors here and in Europe, Asia, and India the following queries:

- Although it may be true that you already have wonderful connections with college administrators, faculty, and students, are your own knowledge, skills, and expertise regarding community issues being fully incorporated into the collaboration?

- Are there individual or organizational aspects of the relationship that don't feel quite reciprocal and need improvement?
- Are you stymied by or uncertain about where to start in developing collaborations with colleges?
- Are there new accountability or assessment pressures you would like to address?
- Do you need a framework to evaluate and guide an improvement process for your agency-college collaboration?

On the basis of hundreds of these conversations and interactions with community partners; reviews of survey, focus group, and narrative data (such as Sandy & Holland, 2006); analysis of anonymous community partner surveys (Plaut et al., 2013); and extensive reading of the research literature, we present here tools and tips for reading and treading the campus terrain in order to equalize the serving and learning playing field.

Specifically, we recommend to you a five-component model and iterative process for community agency partners and their staff who desire to become civic engagement co-educators in initiating, developing, and nurturing community-campus relationships. Although other publications (Cress, Collier, & Reitenauer, 2013; Cress & Donahue, 2011) and on-campus trainings (see, e.g., Office of Academic Innovation, "Teaching Community-Based Courses" workshop, www.pdx.edu/oai) are designed to assist faculty and college students with their roles and responsibilities in community-campus collaborations, this community partner guide is the first of its kind specifically addressed to community partners in promoting their roles as co-educators in the establishment of **effective community-campus relationships that educate students and enhance communities**. It is a guide to empower community partners with tools and techniques for ensuring that such collaborations enrich individuals and organizations alike.

Therefore, as a heuristic structure for mutually educating students and enhancing communities, we offer the *enriching collaborations model* as a framework of strategies for connecting your community agency and yourself with campuses. As will be explicated in the remaining chapters of this guide, the enriching collaborations model describes for community partners how to EXPLORE possibilities, ESTABLISH relationships, ENGAGE faculty, EMPOWER students, and EVALUATE impact (see Figure 1.2) in order to enhance communities.

Enriching collaborations should ultimately produce strengthened educational systems, neighborhoods, and city economies, not to mention improved student learning, skill development, and local-global awareness. In other words, communities and the individuals in those communities are *enhanced*. Yet, fundamental to these outcomes are the core values and processes of reciprocity and equality in civic engagement partnerships that undergird and connect these efforts. Thus, creating the

Figure 1.2.   Enriching collaborations model for enhancing communities.

internal structure and framework for these community-campus relationships is the premise of the model.

Enriching collaborations that fully incorporate community partners as co-educators must be intentionally designed and well tended in order to realize mutual community and campus benefits. In the subsequent chapters (one for each of the model's components), the multitude of methods and techniques offered for consideration and implementation are based on actual campus-college partnerships in the United States and around the world.

As such, the strategies for creating enriching collaborations can be applied to existing campus-college partnerships as a process for honing and *improving* both the service activities and the educational experiences. The information, resources, and materials are intended as a navigation guide for reviewing, revisiting, and revising existing collaborations in an effort to *enhance* their effectiveness, equality, and efficiency for enriching communities.

As well, the ideas and tools are intended for those wishing to initiate and develop new campus-community partnerships. Various approaches and plans are suggested for ensuring that conceptual conversations can be turned into actual learning and serving activities based on mutual understanding, common goals, and reciprocal accountability: in sum, collaborative relationships that enrich both campus and community.

Conclusion

Observantly, Sandy and Holland (2006) noted that higher education institutions and community agencies are not monocultures. Instead, a range of diverse views, motivations, and perceptions of challenges and benefits exist across and within the borders of these organizations. Therefore, application of the enriching collaborations modules should be implemented according to the appropriate values, principles, and objectives associated with each organization.

Still, we assert that the best-practice strategies presented here from real community partner colleagues and premised on proven research literature hold great promise for those desiring to engage themselves as co-educators in forming enriching collaborations. The following chapters detail each of the model's five iterative components: *exploring, establishing, engaging, empowering,* and *evaluating.*

2

EXPLORE POSSIBILITIES

Campus Offices, Clubs, Communities, Courses

Overview: This chapter explores multiple ways of initiating and developing enriching collaborations between the college and the community. Whether the civic engagement relationship is *curricular* (part of a class) or *extracurricular* (not part of a class but supported by the college), *identifying the right person, office, class, or club* will be important to achieving your organization's goals and mission. Therefore, being aware of the wide variety of campus resources can help you be appropriately selective in creating co-educational partnerships.

- Calling on Your Networks for Co-Education
- Connecting With Campus Offices
- Conduits of Connection: AmeriCorps
- College Websites
- Checking in With Clubs
- Convening With Other Campus Communities
- Collaborating With Faculty Courses and Community-Based Research

There are multiple possibilities for enriching collaborations with colleges. You might partner with a community college for a single service day (for instance, as a part of freshman orientation), you might coordinate college seniors from an individual service-learning class each semester, or you might supervise volunteers from a women's sorority such as Kappa Alpha Theta as part of their service requirements.

In West Philadelphia, the Netter Center for Community Partnerships at the University of Pennsylvania has collaborated with schools and local community organizations to create "Partners for Change." The Netter Center houses the Community Schools Student Partnerships (CSSP), a student organization that provides academic and cultural enrichment to children and families across six school districts. CSSP operates recess, school day, after school, and evening programs by recruiting, training, and coordinating over 400 Penn student tutors and mentors. The approach involves tapping community assets of K–12 schools and combining them with the academic and human resources of the university to address challenges.

Based on data collected by the organizations, deliberate attention to the particular needs of each school on the micro-level has led to improved academic performance and classroom behavior for the participating local children. As well, college student academic engagement has increased, and their interest in volunteering in the future has strengthened. On the macro-level, neighborhood stability has improved as a result of decreased truancy and increased high school graduation rates. In turn, the university has realized increased enrollment of new freshmen from the participating school districts.

This community-campus collaboration illustrates what can happen with deep and lasting relationships in which multiple stakeholders integrate their work to solve community issues. Certainly, they illustrate the positive characteristics of enriching collaborations.

But how do these kinds of collaborative efforts get started? And how are community partners able to position themselves as co-educators in their work with college campuses? This chapter will explore these questions and provide practical guidance for navigating college bureaucracies in efforts to establish long-term relationships that can enhance and transform communities.

Calling on Your Networks for Co-Education

Work your network

Perhaps the simplest way to reach out to potential campus partners is through your own network. Maybe you already have relationships at the college: A faculty member who serves on your advisory board might suggest other colleagues for a collaborative community-based research project. Or existing college student volunteers could recommend an open-minded faculty member for a new senior-level capstone project to help you redesign your website based on a community needs survey.

On the professional level, you may have community service, nonprofit, and agency colleagues who are collaborating with colleges. Can they suggest an individual or office that might get you started? Or on the personal level, is there any chance that you have a neighbor who works at the local college? Perhaps this is the perfect opportunity to invite him or her over for a cup of coffee so you can get to know each other better and brainstorm possible networks of connection.

Network with colleagues and acquaintances

Even if you don't think that your current contact is a person with whom you ultimately want to partner, he or she may be able to provide you with the name of an individual or campus office that might be able to help. Better yet, he or she might be willing to make an introduction, such as sending an e-mail to connect you with the campus service-learning director.

Consider This Real-Life Networking Example: At an after-school program for at-risk youth, the volunteer coordinator mentioned that she wanted to start working with college volunteers. It turned out that one of the teachers in the program was married to a professor in the engineering department, so she offered to arrange a meeting. The volunteer coordinator wasn't looking for tutors in engineering, but the professor knew of faculty colleagues who might be interested and provided her with contact information.

Of course, as you call on your network and converse about your desire to create an enriching community-campus collaboration, you have the opportunity to set the tone in your role as a co-educator. As such, articulate not just what your organization *needs* but also what your organization can *offer*.

- What might students *learn* if they assist your program?
- What *knowledge* might they gain about a particular discipline or subject area?
- What *skills* might they gain for a chosen profession or career?
- What *insights* might they gain regarding personal strengths, values, attitudes, or character?

Take a tip from a human rights organization in Portland, Oregon: Create volunteer positions or internships that include an academic major or related field in the title such as "graphic design internship," "after-school educational program coordinator," "marketing intern," or "computer support volunteer."

Include an academic major in the position title

Similarly, if you are working with an instructor or faculty member as part of a class project or service-learning relationship, suggest how your own expertise and that of your staff can contribute to the academic experience of the college students. You may have articles or book chapters to offer as possible assignments or websites that could be reviewed by students to familiarize them with key concepts and information about your clients or community.

Questions to Consider When Exploring Possibilities as a Co-Educator:

- What are the academic dimensions of your work? Are there readings or research in your field or about the community issues that you could contribute?
- What in your work will help students learn or better understand their course material?
- What new skills might students gain by working with your organization?
- What in your work will help students' career development?
- What might students learn about themselves by working with your organization?
- What can you share about your own experience that might be interesting or important for students to know?

An important structural feature to understand of most campuses is how the various departments, offices, and centers are arranged within the bureaucratic hierarchy of the institution. Typically, the two primary organizational categories at colleges and universities are *academic affairs* and *student affairs*. You may encounter a third organizational unit, *business affairs*, which can include areas like the alumni office or foundations director.

Academic affairs generally includes all departments and organizational units on campus related to the curriculum and degrees (majors and minors) offered at that college, as well as offices that support those programs. For example, the chemistry department, library, and registrar typically fall under academic affairs. Although the college president or chancellor is usually the leader of the entire institution, the provost, vice president, or dean of academic affairs is primarily concerned with academic programs and personnel.

In contrast, student affairs includes offices that support the overall college experience for students and provides what are termed "co-curricular learning opportunities and activities." Residence life, student activities, and clubs are areas commonly within student affairs. Usually, a dean of student life or vice president of student affairs manages these areas.

The distinction between these two organizational units is important because understanding "which side of the house" you are working with can shape how you articulate and frame the co-education opportunities you offer. For example, faculty and staff in **academic affairs are probably most interested in partnerships that further students' academic learning and intellectual growth**, such as a collaboration between the English department and a local literacy program as part of a service-learning course. **Alternatively, student affairs professionals might be more interested in opportunities for leadership development or social bonding among students.** For instance, a residence hall director might want to organize a weekend "service day" to help students get to know each other as they provide community assistance.

It is hoped your network contacts will offer guidance on language, jargon, terminology, and acronyms that you might use (or not) when calling on their referrals. Indeed, don't be surprised if a faculty member asks you, **"Why should I take time out of my course for students to volunteer?"** Although we will discuss myriad strategies for working with faculty in chapter 4, we encourage you to state at the outset to instructors what students might learn. Similarly, you may decide to contact the women's resource center to find volunteers to assist your women in transition program. Describe to the center director the interpersonal communication training that you will offer to participating students. (See chapter 5 for more ideas on empowering students as a co-educator.)

Although reaching out to your various networks for college contact suggestions is a great place to start in exploring campus possibilities, some of their recommended paths may not lead to successful connections. In fact, you may get lost or become confused by wrong e-mail addresses, phone numbers, and relocated offices. As such, whether you are following a clearly marked campus map of contacts given to you by a friend or striking out on your own through the wilderness of college centers, you will find the following strategies helpful for connecting with campus offices, clubs, and departments.

> "I never considered using the bilingual skills of international students! Of course, now it makes perfect sense for our Refugee and Immigrant Center!"

Connecting With Campus Offices

Traversing the maze of institutional bureaucratic offices can be daunting. A voice mail may go unreturned, an e-mail can bounce back, an unfriendly receptionist may disconnect your call, or an instructor may tersely suggest to "come to my office hours if you want to talk to me."

What's in a Name? Examples of Various Offices Doing Similar Work at Different Institutions:

- Office of Community-University Partnerships (Rutgers-Newark)
- Center for Civic Engagement (University of Texas-Brownsville)
- Office of Community Service-Learning (Willamette University)

- Center for Learning Through Service (Anne Arundel Community College)
- Center for Engagement With Communities (Whittier College)
- Office of Community Engagement and Service (Miami University)
- Office of Volunteer Programs (University of Illinois)
- Office of Experiential Education and Civic Engagement (Kent State)
- Office of Service-Learning and Community Action (Emerson College)
- Center for Public Service (Tulane University)
- Collaborative for Community Engagement (Colorado College)

Like many large organizations, the individual units within campuses can often feel quite disconnected, with staff that may or may not know what is happening in the building next door or how to appropriately refer you to the correct person. It may take persistence on your part to find someone who can really be helpful in answering your questions or meeting your needs.

To make matters more complicated, not only do individual institutions organize their units dissimilarly, but if a college has multiple campuses (perhaps in various regions of the city or with specific academic specialties), there may be different structures or names for offices that have primary responsibility for managing community partnerships. In addition, there may be multiple offices with overlapping responsibility for varying kinds of community partnerships (such as volunteering or service-learning courses).

The following sections describe numerous offices and their basic delineations to help you through the organizational matrix.

Volunteer Office

Perhaps you need a group of students to assist with your annual auction on a Saturday evening from 6:00 p.m. to 10:00 p.m. The volunteer office may be able to help. A volunteer office assists students in creating or finding community service opportunities. This kind of unit can be run by college professional staff or by student staff and be part of or separate from the other offices described next.

Centers or Offices for Civic Engagement or Service-Learning

Maybe you would like to develop an ongoing partnership in which students majoring in social work conduct the intake interviews at your homeless shelter. The center for service-learning may be able to connect you to the right faculty member to develop a course-based partnership.

Offices or centers of service-learning or civic engagement focus on connecting campus and community through activities that enhance academic learning. Typically staffed by an academic professional or faculty member, these offices may have student interns or work-study students who coordinate placements or act as liaisons with community partners. These units may also provide the same services as that of a volunteer office. As well, these centers usually provide assistance to faculty implementing a service-learning course (such as conducting faculty workshops on how to integrate community service into their syllabi and assignments).

At California State University, Monterey Bay, the Service Learning Institute serves as an instructional unit, academic resource center, center for developing community partnerships, and home of the student leadership program. The institute offers an online Community Partner Guide for those exploring possibilities with the campus (http://service.csumb.edu/community-partner-guide). The institute also conducts Community Partner Orientation sessions each semester to familiarize potential partners with the process and philosophical and pedagogical trainings for developing realistic expectations and gaining effective student supervisory and learning facilitation strategies.

> Check with your local college(s) to see if there are online Community Partner Resources or a Community Partner Orientation session that you can attend.

Offices or Centers of Academic Excellence or Teaching Effectiveness

Maybe students from the education department have provided activities for children at your domestic violence shelter, but you would like to expand student roles in working with mothers and other women. To do so, you feel that a formal service-learning course would best prepare students' knowledge and interpersonal skills. Because many colleges do not have an official office of community engagement or service-learning, you may need to explore possibilities with the office of academic excellence or teaching effectivness.

Student Activities or Student Life

Perhaps you received a call from staff in the orientation office that want to partner with you for Freshman Service Day. The orientation office is charged with welcoming new students to campus, providing both the resources they need to get off to a good start and a strong social foundation. A growing number of orientation programs include some kind of community service component, which ranges from an optional cleanup project on a single morning (e.g., picking up trash along a river) to a required daylong event including a host of different projects with multiple organizations (e.g., painting over graffiti at a school or assisting with home building for low-income families).

Orientation and Freshman Service Day is just one example of programs offered under student affairs. Others may include an alternative spring break (when students volunteer at a service site for an entire week) or Martin Luther King Jr. Day of Service.

Also, offices of student activities (also referred to as *student life*) provide enrichment activities for special populations. For example, at the University of California-Irvine, the Office of Student Life and Leadership coordinates programs for groups such as the Lesbian Gay Bisexual Transgender Resource Center and the International Student Center. Similarly, the Office of Student Activities at Howard University provides first-generation students (those who are the first in their family to attend college) with ways to get involved with community service as a form of leadership development.

Depending on how a college is structured, these types of offices might be your best strategy for exploring a potential campus relationship, especially if you don't have a referral from a friend or colleague. However, there are a variety of other college offices and centers that you might want to consider contacting.

Career Services

Are you the kind of person who knew exactly what you wanted to do in life and then did it, or did your career path have a few more twists and turns? On college campuses, offices of career services or career development support students' professional development, including conducting a job search after graduation, preparing a résumé, and getting interview coaching. Offices like the Albright College Experiential Learning and Career Development Center support volunteer placement, as well as internships and service-learning, with the idea that these kinds of experiences promote career development. As mentioned earlier, consider developing a position description to post in the career center, whether paid or unpaid, if you are seeking a few student volunteers or service interns. Another idea is to attend and represent your organization at a campus career fair. If you are a nonprofit, the college may offer reduced fees for the opportunity to educate students (and faculty and administrators) about your agency's mission and services.

Go to the
career fair

Of course, the differences and nuances of responsibilities among offices with similar names can be perplexing. For instance, at Clarion University the Career Services Center has responsibility for Community Service Work-Study, which is a federal program that utilizes work-study funds to pay for student workers in community organizations. In contrast, Community Service Work-Study is administered by the Bonner Center for Service and Learning at Oberlin College and by the Financial Aid Office at Vassar College.

> *Important Information:* Any college that accepts federal work-study funds is obligated to ensure that a certain percentage of those funds is spent in the community. This is a great way for students to get paid for work done in a community organization while helping the college meet a federal obligation.

As you consider what you might be able to offer students and your campus partners, think about your own career trajectory, your current profession, and the kinds of jobs involved with fulfilling your organization's mission. **Highlighting the skills and knowledge** that students will gain when you are partnering with a campus office can be particularly productive for everyone involved. It may be that your description leads you to an office you never considered, such as the Advancement or Development Office.

Highlight skills and knowledge students will gain

Community-University Relations, College Advancement, and Development Office

Perhaps you have a grant opportunity that requires partnership among multiple nonprofit organizations, NGOs, or government agencies. College offices such as the Advancement or Development Office promote the campus for purposes of public relations and fund-raising. Though typically these offices are not directly involved with service-learning collaborations on the day-to-day level, they may be eager to showcase partnerships, support cooperative grant-seeking efforts, or track the number and types of organizations the campus works with. They may also have good connections with media outlets to draw attention to service-oriented events or programs.

Consider This Real-Life Collaboration: An after-school program for at-risk students at a middle school sought to reapply for the private foundation grant that supported its program. Many students from the nearby liberal arts college volunteered at the after-school program, conducting such activities as a spoken-word workshop, intramural soccer, and a homework club. The after-school program coordinator asked the college's development director to write a letter of support highlighting the partnership between the school and the college. The foundation sponsored another 3-year grant for the collaboration.

There is strength in numbers (i.e., enriching collaborations), and most grant-issuing agencies and foundations realize this fact. The same is true for college faculty and administrators. In addition to the learning that may be gained by students or the service provided to the community, the opportunity to obtain additional fiscal resources can be a tantalizing enticement for college personnel. Moreover, it is often the case that faculty career advancement is contingent on faculty members' ability to secure grant monies. *Thus, in addition to articulating the knowledge and skills that can be gained through community-campus collaborations, you may want to* **outline the potential fiscal resources** *that could be mutually realized.*

Outline the potential fiscal resources

Conduits of Connection: AmeriCorps

Another way to connect with a campus may be through an **AmeriCorps member or representative**. AmeriCorps is a federal program in which members are placed at various organizations for a fixed period of time (typically 9 months, a year, or a set number of hours) with a focused position targeted around a particular need in the community. There are several variations of AmeriCorps, such as AmeriCorps VISTA, which is an antipoverty program, or AmeriCorps State and National, which includes projects related to education, disaster relief, and health.

With over 75,000 members serving nationwide, AmeriCorps is perhaps the largest service program in the country, although other service corps programs exist, such as the Jesuit Volunteer Corps and Student Conservation Association. AmeriCorps members receive a nominal stipend to cover basic living expenses but are not considered employees of their host organization.

Often, AmeriCorps positions are created with the specific intent of relationship building between community agencies and college offices. Whether working for the college or a community partner, service corps members may undertake such tasks as developing volunteer recruitment materials, creating a partnership plan, writing a program manual, or outlining the structure of a new collaborative program.

As such, don't be surprised (or confused) if you are contacted by an AmeriCorps member calling from a college office of service-learning to explore collaboration possibilities, for example, on your housing assistance program for people transitioning out of homelessness. The AmeriCorps member may be able to arrange an information meeting on campus, create flyers, or meet with you every other week to coordinate details in a way that a faculty or staff member on campus rarely has time to do.

Because it is never the intent of programs such as AmeriCorps to replace full-time staff or develop programs that become dependent on the AmeriCorps position, over time members' roles may shift toward implementing systems that can be sustained by permanent staff. Service corps members, therefore, present an excellent resource and opportunity for innovation and collaborative planning for long-term success. As such, you may also find them located in a variety of campus offices such as admissions, financial aid, or student activities.

College Websites

Search the college website

If visiting campus offices or cold-calling an AmeriCorps member is still too confusing, the college website may be a helpful resource to explore before initiating any communications. Doing keyword searches or perusing the different drop-down menus may provide you with clues about the services offered by a particular office or whether an individual contact person seems promising (for instance, you can review faculty members'

Try using combinations of these words in a key word search on the college website:

- volunteer
- service, service-learning
- civic engagement, civic learning
- partner, partnerships
- community service
- community engagement
- collaboration
- office, center
- director, coordinator
- AmeriCorps, VISTA

web pages to see the courses that they teach or their research interests). Depending on the institution, web pages may be kept more or less current. Another option might be to call the institution's primary contact number (main phone line) and ask the operator to be connected to the community engagement center (then hope for the best!).

Checking in With Clubs

Student clubs are an excellent source of volunteers because they are inherently social in nature and often seek activities for their group. In fact, some clubs have service as a required responsibility for their members. Thus, whether for a onetime service project or an ongoing commitment, consider building a relationship with a student club. Although most student clubs have potential as volunteer groups, targeting select student clubs that are preprofessional, interest based, and advocacy oriented can be particularly fruitful.

Preprofessional Clubs

Preprofessional clubs are composed of students with an interest in a specific career or profession. Most often, students are eager to gain experience in that field. The pre-med club might be interested in serving at a health fair, for example, or the pre-law club might want to strike up a partnership with a local legal clinic. Virtually all preprofessional clubs have a faculty adviser who may be a potential contact. As well, some fields have honor societies. Phi Kappa Phi is an honor society for all academic disciplines, and the Rho Chi Society is for students in the field of pharmacology.

Interest-Based Clubs

Interest-based clubs bring students together around a common interest, perhaps related to their academic pursuits, cultural backgrounds, or individual hobbies. The biology club might be interested in an invasive species removal project that connects interests in nature and ecology. The international club might be able to provide the sets of hands you need for a festival celebrating the local Somali immigrant population. The computer science club might be interested in helping you revamp your website.

Advocacy- and Service-Oriented Clubs

Advocacy- and service-oriented clubs tap existing passions of students to take action and serve their communities. Groups such as Circle K, the Community Service Club, or the Rainbow Coalition might already have special events or activities to which they devote their time, but even these events can be an opportunity to partner or advertise your work.

For example, the student club Colleges Against Cancer might have an annual fund-raiser that it works on, but with a bit of collective effort, you could find a way for your group to share information at the event. Perhaps the Colleges Against

Cancer student organizers would be willing to put a stack of your brochures at the registration table regarding free health care screenings for elders or allow you to pass out pamphlets to the crowd.

Other service-oriented clubs might be interested in promoting animal welfare, advocating for the civil rights of sexual minorities, or raising awareness about environmental issues. Because these students are predisposed to get involved, they could make great partners for your project.

College websites often have a relatively current listing of student clubs. Because of the frequent turnover of leaders and evolving student interests, however, the website may not be current. For example, at a public 4-year university in the Midwest, Food Rescue is a student-led initiative. Students work together to prevent food waste at the institution and encourage redistribution of food to those in need in the greater community. Two years ago, four of the five students who initiated the project graduated. The remaining member could not solicit enough effort on her own to keep the group going last year. But this year a new set of students from the environmental studies department has expressed interest in reviving the student club. Thus, your own efforts for connecting with student clubs may wax and wane as individual students enter and leave the institution. Still, there is usually a student affairs professional staff member responsible for oversight of student clubs. It may be that your sustained relationship is with this individual rather than with the student club or its members.

Convening With Other Campus Communities

Besides student clubs, other communities of students exist for convening and exploring common purposes. Indeed, some require student community service as an aspect of membership.

Greek Organizations

Perhaps you attended a college with fraternities and sororities, the Greek organizations common at many institutions. Not all campuses have a Greek system (known by the Greek letters forming their names), and they vary in number and influence on campus culture. Among those that do, though, they are likely to have some community involvement commitment. In some cases, service or charity work is a requirement of a national chartering body.

For example, members of the Theta Chi fraternity are strongly encouraged to support one of the national network's preferred philanthropies, which are listed on its web page and include the National Bone Marrow Registry and the Starlight Children's Foundation. As another illustration, students at a university in the southern United States from the sorority Delta Chi Delta selected the Susan G. Komen Foundation as their charity for engaging in activities to raise awareness and funds for breast cancer.

Fraternity or sorority members could be a great group to support a fund-raiser or to adopt your organization to volunteer on a regular basis. Checking the college's student life website or asking current student volunteers about whether there is a Greek system at their school could be good places to start.

Residence Halls

If you attended college, you might remember the dorm as much as you do your courses—and you wouldn't be alone! Residence halls are a central point of student life on residential campuses. Whether the residence hall is a traditional dormitory-style building that brings random students together or a thematic floor (e.g., environmental sustainability) that students have chosen to live on, students in residence halls are another campus community that might be interested in working with your organization. Staff or student leaders may want to build bonds in their living community through interaction with the outside community. What better opportunity than a service project?

> "The elder residents were delighted to chat with students and point out places they had 'missed' painting. For days following, the residents talked with one another about the visit, so the walls as well as hearts and minds were brightened."

Many colleges also have specialized housing opportunities, such as an eco-house, an international floor, or a Spanish-language house. Oberlin College targets its Sustainability Hall and Student Experiment in Ecological Design (SEED House) toward first-year students. EcoHouse is a living-learning community at the University of Connecticut. In these environments students have chosen to integrate their interests into their lifestyle, and as such, they might be good candidates for collaboration.

Example Collaboration: A private, religiously affiliated college (which requires freshmen and sophomores to live on campus) had a college-wide day of community service. Students from the Spanish floor of a residence hall chose to serve at an elder community center occupied primarily by Latino and Latina senior citizens. The students conversed in Spanish with the elders while they painted the garden fence. At the same location, students from the Environmental House (residence hall) weeded invasive species and put in native plants on the grounds.

As you explore becoming a co-educator in civic engagement, consider what might be of interest to groups such as these. Do you have a new "green" building to show students who want to learn about sustainability? Do you have a nice picnic

Consider the group's interest

area where the students from a residence hall could bring bag lunches to reflect and socialize after their project?

If you are interested in getting connected with residence halls or houses, your best bet is to contact the office of residence life or the college's volunteer office. Institutions are not likely to give out student information directly, so you may need to rely on them to spread the word and have interested students contact you.

Athletic Teams

When you think about college sports, you might imagine tailgate parties or big televised national tournaments. These days, though, many college teams are becoming involved with service, in addition to their area of competition. As illustration, Ron Hunter, who coached for such prominent men's college basketball teams as Georgia State and Indiana University-Purdue University Indianapolis (IUPUI), has also earned a reputation for his humanitarian efforts providing shoes to children. By partnering with the U.S.-based organization Samaritan's Feet, his players and fans have donated over 250,000 pairs of shoes to date.

Indeed, athletic departments at colleges across the country are engaging in community service work. Teams routinely serve the community by coaching at youth camps, hosting clinics to help kids learn the game, and working at Habitat for Humanity, park cleanups, and homeless shelters. Sometimes these activities take place in the off-season as a way to keep the team connected, whereas at other times they happen in the midst of the season to develop teamwork or simply to put school spirit to good use at its peak.

Connect with athletic directors and coaches

Connecting with athletic directors and individual coaches is a good way to reach out to athletic teams. If you already have student volunteers, ask if they participate in a college sport. Similarly, just in case the captain of the swim club sends you an e-mail asking about doing a half-day service project for the team, explore your options.

Collaborating With Faculty Courses and Community-Based Research

Collaboration Example: Amanda supervises volunteers at the local food bank, which includes a community garden. They need help each fall harvesting produce, preparing food boxes, cleaning up the garden beds, and creating educational materials about nutrition to be inserted into every food box. As she was already busy recruiting volunteers for the warehouse, Amanda wanted to find a group to come back year after year to the community garden. After she heard a segment on the news about the local community college service day, it hit her—maybe someone on campus could help. After calling the college's office of service and civic engagement, she learned that a faculty member in the biology department had been looking for a partner for a nutrition class that runs every fall. It was the perfect fit!

Building relationships with courses and faculty creates an excellent opportunity for deeply integrative and sustained collaborations in which you truly become a co-educator of students. In addition to working through your own network, contacting academic departments and singling out individual course faculty can be a productive way to explore a partnership.

Academic Departments

Developing relationships with academic departments can be useful, particularly on campuses that lack a centralized office such as a center for service-learning. Departments such as the biology department, art department, or anthropology department manage the curriculum and provide the organizational unit for most faculty. Although academic departments are not likely to be involved with activities that are strictly volunteer in nature, they are often interested in opportunities to enhance their students' learning and may have strong commitments to social justice, equity, community engagement, or applied learning outside of the classroom.

For example, many sociology departments are explicit in their promotional materials and website that faculty are committed to social justice or that they encourage a social justice perspective, indicating that this might be a good set of people to involve in your human rights campaign. Likewise, if a chemistry department notes its commitment to applied learning, then perhaps faculty in that department would be interested in having their students test streams in the local watershed for pollutants.

Sometimes, working directly with the department chair in an academic department can provide consistency if multiple faculty teach the same community-based learning course. In addition, on some campuses faculty will help students identify and secure internships or placements for service-learning requirements. If possible, see if the college, department, or program website contains a list of service-learning, community-based learning, or applied learning courses.

Other academic departments that may be especially willing to explore community-campus collaborations are such fields as social work, education, anthropology, psychology, and urban studies. Also, depending on the types of populations you serve, you may also want to contact the foreign languages department and their affiliated programs in

> *BUS 330: Business Ethics in Action:* In this course, students explore their professional aspirations and ethical values. They develop respect for multiple perspectives through community reflections. They integrate business concepts with service-learning components. This learning takes place in the context of community development in the county area with a minimum of 30 service hours.
>
> *COMM 426: Creative Writing and Service:* This course develops service-learning sensitivity and creative writing competency and craft. Students develop original pieces and age-appropriate interdisciplinary creative projects for service-learning partners in the schools.

Consider working with the department chair

Spanish, Vietnamese, or Thai. Finally, be aware of multidisciplinary programs such as international relations, foreign relations, or conflict mediation that may house faculty and students interested in local-global service needs and issues.

Faculty and Courses

In some cases, collaborations may be established through individual faculty member courses. Depending on the campus, full-time faculty (assistant, associate, or full professors) may teach 4 to 12 courses each academic year. The number of courses is dependent on additional expectations such as publishing, presenting, grant writing, advising, and other administrative tasks (see also chapter 4). Instructors who are adjunct (meaning part-time) are paid on a course-by-course basis (usually without health or retirement benefits). Adjunct faculty may teach 1 to 6 courses on a single campus.

Usually a list of current courses is publicly available on the institution's website, and courses may have a special designation as service-learning or community-based learning. Try searching for terms such as "course catalog" or "current course" for a downloadable publication or searchable database of class offerings. Contacting the instructor, who is often listed with course information, directly can be an efficient way of exploring collaborations; however, be aware that faculty are notorious for not returning unsolicited calls and e-mail!

Do your homework

Therefore, do your homework before contacting a faculty member. First, scan the college catalog or website for possible courses. Second, identify the **knowledge** and **skills** that such a collaboration with this course would develop.

For example, if you need assistance with your website, look up computer science courses and read the differences between an introductory and an advanced web design class. If available, review the syllabus to give you insights about how service at your organization can help students learn the content.

As well, imagine that you want a YouTube video link on your website to highlight community needs and assets that your organization addresses and for which you are trying to recruit volunteers. In perusing the semester course listings, you come across a class titled "Social Change Through Film." Before excitedly e-mailing the professor, outline how your organization creates social change and how students can apply their *content knowledge* and *film skills* in a mutual collaboration.

Sample Service-Learning Courses and Departments:

- Social Ethics (Philosophy)
- Child Development (Psychology)
- Introduction to Spanish (World Languages)
- Speech Communication (Communication)
- Marriage and Family (Sociology)
- Arts and Community Development (Art)

- Sustainability in Urban Communities (Landscape Architecture)
- Companion Animal Science (Biology)
- College Writing (English)
- Engineering in Urban Education

Faculty Community-Based Research

In addition to identifying faculty courses, another option is to tap faculty research interests. In many institutions—though not all—faculty are expected to conduct research in addition to teaching. If they have an individual web page, their publications and research reports may be listed, which can indicate the kinds of topics they research (also known as their "scholarly agenda"). (We will explore more ideas for community-based assessment and impact research in chapter 4.)

> *Case Example:* A Spanish instructor at a large university had not only expertise in language instruction but researched and published on the effects of peer tutoring in language acquisition. The coordinator of a bilingual after-school program learned of this research from a colleague at a local nonprofit alliance breakfast meeting. The coordinator made a cold call to the professor, who agreed to meet for coffee. They decided to collaborate on a research project to examine effectiveness of college student tutors on developing high school students' Spanish- and English-language competence. The professor's research goals were met, the college students got great experience in language instruction, and the high school students had tutoring based on tested methods that ended up improving their language scores.

Worth noting is that faculty—like any other group—are more or less responsive and communicative. It can indeed be exasperating to find just the right person (you think) to partner with, only to wait with disappointment for your voice message to be returned. The bottom line is this: If your communication is not reciprocated, you did not find the right person!

Undergraduate Student Community-Based Research

Related to collaborating with faculty on community-based research, individual students may be interested and willing to assist your organization with survey design, distribution, and analysis; focus groups or interviews; document analysis; or report writing. In fact, some colleges like Whittier have an annual Undergraduate Research, Scholarship, and Creative Activities presentation day to highlight community-based research work conducted by students. Similarly, the University of California, Los Angeles, sponsors two undergraduate research centers to help define students' academic interests and improve research skills: Undergraduate Research Center for the Arts, Humanities, and Social Sciences and Undergraduate Research Center: Sciences.

Graduate Student Community-Based Research

Students working on their master's thesis or doctoral dissertations may also be looking for sites to research or collect data. Probably your best contact source is the academic department chair or faculty adviser in a graduate program. Alternatively, you may have existing data waiting to be analyzed and interpreted. Often graduate students have advanced research skills that could assist your agency.

Be honest

Perhaps most important of all these ideas, if you get in touch with a person who seems *not to be the right one*, be honest and ask for another referral. As frustrating and time-consuming as this process can be, eventually you will find someone who can help you develop the collaboration you seek. Consider the real illustration in the following case example.

> *Case Example:* In the Pacific Northwest, a rural animal rescue operator was interested in hosting student volunteers to care for the animals. She had managed to reach someone at the financial aid office of the local college through the friend of a friend. The staff member in financial aid who took the message passed it along to a social work faculty member, who in turn sent it to an associate dean. The associate dean sent it to the director of the Center for Civic Engagement, who returned the call, learned more about the animal rescue operation, and then was able to help recruit students in an animal ethics class in the philosophy department and the animal rights club to volunteer.

Of course, any of these processes can work in reverse as well. Rather than having to seek out students or campus personnel, you might find that they come to you. Perhaps a faculty member contacts you after attending a conference at which he saw a presentation about service-learning and decides he wants to bring his class to your organization every week during the spring semester. Or you could receive a call from a student across the country (or world) who will be visiting your city for an alternative spring break. Upon further conversation, she explains that an alternative spring break is a service-based program in which students contribute to a cause rather than take a vacation over spring break. She conducted a Google search and found your organization, hoping that you could provide a service project for 10 students during the week.

Have multiple tentative conversations

In both cases, you might be caught off guard or think that you won't be able to help them. Or maybe it was just the call you've been waiting for! Either way, take time to explore the relationship before settling on any agreements. **Having multiple tentative conversations is a good way to build a strong foundation for enriching collaborations.** Talk about what you and your counterpart need and what you each can offer. Discuss logistical details, such as schedules or paperwork, and articulate your goals and expectations. It's also perfectly acceptable to decline such requests, though you may suggest that a different time, another project, or perhaps someone else at your organization might work better and go from there. (In chapter 3, we offer even more strategies for conversation starters and relationship building.)

> *Case Example:* At a small public school just down the street from a liberal arts college, the principal felt rather obliged to accept all college student volunteers. She had made friends with various faculty over the years so was reluctant to voice her frustrations over some of the impositions. Eventually, she confided in a trusted colleague. The professor suggested that she have an honest conversation with the community engagement director. She did, and together they strategized what programs and courses made the most sense for the school and the college. By speaking up, she was able to strengthen the partnership and transition from being a "student volunteer scheduler" to a co-educator in college student learning.

Conclusion

Enriching collaborations start with thoughtful explorations in order to identify the soundest connections. By framing, early on, these potential collaborations from a position of co-education—the knowledge and skills you can provide students—you can create a relationship more likely to flourish in common understanding and trust. In the following chapter, we recommend myriad specific strategies for *establishing relationships* as reciprocal, mutually beneficial, and sustainable; in essence, collaborations that enrich the personal and professional lives of everyone involved.

3

ESTABLISH RELATIONSHIPS

Characteristics, Contexts, Culture, Common Agreements

Overview: This chapter introduces the building blocks for mutually beneficial *reciprocal* relationships between the college and the community. Studies have shown that these collaborations can benefit all parties, if they are implemented carefully and with an understanding of the *context* and *culture* of both the community and the college. Anticipating everyone's needs and addressing them in advance through *common agreements* can help ensure positive collaborations.

- Characteristics and Contexts of Enriching Collaborations
- Crossing Cultural Boundaries
- Common Agreements

"I call on all Americans to stand up and do what they can to serve their communities, shape our history, and enrich both their own lives and the lives of others across this country."

—President Barack Obama, March 2009

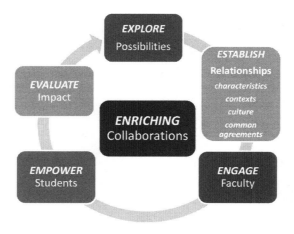

Characteristics and Contexts of Enriching Collaborations

Over two decades of research on campus-community collaborations has established that service-learning and civic engagement activities are effective strategies for student growth and community improvement (Astin, Sax, & Avalos, 1999; Battistoni, Longo, & Jayanandhan, 2009; Bernackiand & Jaeger, 2008; Cress, Yamashita, Duarte, & Burns, 2010; Eyler & Giles, 1999; Sandy & Holland, 2006; Vogelgesang, 2004).

Civic engagement activities

- increase student retention and graduation rates,
- increase future volunteerism, and
- increase the social and economic vitality of communities.

Given our national and international interdependence, there has never been a more urgent and catalytic time to connect campuses with communities (Cress, Burack, Giles, Elkins, & Stevens, 2010) to create more socially equitable and sustainable towns, cities, states, and nations (Colby, Ehrlich, Beaumont, & Stephens, 2003). Quintessentially, lives and communities are transformed even if just one teenager decides to remain in high school and forgo gang activity.

But what do we mean by *enriching collaborations*? And what are the *characteristic outcomes* of such collaborations?

- Campuses are enhanced:
  - Students learn more academic content by examining disciplinary concepts and applying their knowledge to community challenges.
  - Students gain interpersonal and intercultural skills by interacting with diverse classmates and communities.
  - Faculty expand research and scholarship by investigating new sources of data and community expertise.

- Communities are improved:
  - Individuals are empowered to act and advocate for themselves.
  - Organizational efficiency and capacity are increased.
  - Health, educational, social, economic, and environmental assets are strengthened.

The context for such partnerships is referred to as *reciprocal relationships* or *reciprocity*. O'Meara and Rice (2005) defined reciprocity as a genuine collaboration that is multidirectional in the sharing of expertise and benefits. Perhaps you have been involved in a service-learning partnership with two different colleges in your city. With one college, you feel respected as a partner, and your collaboration seems to continually improve—even though you've had some serious challenges to work through. Together you have developed a system for engaging students that is productive for all involved. Certainly, these are characteristics of reciprocity.

However, the other campus partnership feels more like a strain—you are rarely asked for feedback about how hosting students is working for you, and there are ongoing unresolved tensions around scheduling issues and mismatches between what students say they are required to do and what you are able to provide for them. This does not feel like a reciprocal relationship.

Ideally, reciprocity at the organizational level is an equal exchange of benefits between both the college and the community. As well, at the individual level, reciprocity implies a mutuality of common goals, shared accountability, and positively realized outcomes for students, faculty, community partners, and community recipients (or clients).

With these characteristics and context in mind, Furco (1999) designed a framework for higher education institutions to initiate, develop, and sustain reciprocal community partnerships. Fundamentally, faculty and college administrators who are working with community partners should strive in their relationships to integrate three primary components: *awareness, mutual understanding,* and *leadership and voice.*

1. *Awareness:* Community agencies are aware of campus goals for civic engagement and the range of opportunities available.
2. *Mutual understanding:* Campus and community representatives understand each other's needs, timelines, resources, and capacity for implementing activities, and there is general agreement regarding mutual goals.
3. *Leadership and voice:* Agency representatives are encouraged to advocate on campus for civic engagement, express their community's needs, and recruit faculty and student participation.

Of course, these laudable goals may be more idealistic than realistic. Community partners may have no *awareness* that a faculty member is motivated simply because the dean or department chair suggested that community service would be valuable for that faculty's vitae (résumé). Students may have no *understanding* of the community agency's goals because they never took time to review the website. Community partners may feel *voiceless* in articulating their organization's needs for fear of losing volunteers. Moreover, it is quite likely that none of the collaborators (faculty, students, or community partners) have ever heard of the Furco Higher Education Rubric for Reciprocal Partnerships!

> "Students helped with logistical support, volunteer management, and social media. These efforts increased the numbers of our elder lunch program."

> **Community Partner:** "The col-
> laboration was instrumental in
> reaching ethnic and low-income
> communities, including services
> for teenage mothers, gang and
> crime prevention, and building
> the capacity of our staff from
> diverse populations."

Thus, once you have identified a campus contact through your explorations of possibilities, it will probably be up to you as a co-educator to *inquire* about campus, department, or course goals; to *describe* your organization's capacity and needs to ensure student and faculty understanding; and to continue to *vocalize* your thoughts and feelings about how things are going (or where you want them to go!).

In many ways, reciprocal community-campus collaborations should demonstrate "essential features of genuine democratic partnerships" (Jacoby, 2003, p. 9). After all, the inherent purpose of most civic engagement activities is to expose students to the responsibilities and opportunities of living and working in a democratic society.

As Cress and Donahue (2011) pointed out, democracy is a grand experiment in balancing individual rights with mutual concerns and in negotiating conflicting values with common principles. In short, our most important educational challenge is to teach equitable inclusion of every member of society in the midst of inequitable organizations and systems while working to right those injustices.

So what does this mean in real terms? **The nature of community service and service-learning experiences is messy.** Civic engagement is messy because it involves diverse personalities, perspectives, and backgrounds. Civic engagement is messy because it involves real people grappling with real-life issues. Indeed, it is the complications, controversies, and dilemmas of service-learning that offer the most "teachable" moments for all involved.

Case Example: Professor Heather taught "introductory nutrition" at Multnomah Community College and arranged with the principal of a local middle school for her students to assist at their community garden. The community college students were supervised by a volunteer from the parent-teacher association (PTA), and they conducted outreach in the neighborhood to inform families about the upcoming garden harvest festival, recruit volunteers to help with the event, and raise awareness about children's nutrition by going door-to-door in the neighborhood.

However, after just two afternoons of outreach, the students expressed severe frustration to Professor Heather. Very few people were home, and those who did answer closed their door as soon as they found out they were working with the PTA. Others did not speak English and gave a blank look when the students showed them the gardening information pamphlet.

Professor Heather called the school principal, who revealed that there had recently been a contentious meeting at the PTA concerning lack of sensitivity in working with the neighborhood's growing immigrant population. The principal admitted that she did not realize how bad the situation had become.

Professor Heather had a class discussion to process students' frustrations, provide background about neighborhood dynamics, and collaboratively develop new strategies. The students decided to focus their outreach on nutrition education and the organic garden. Students translated the informational pamphlet into Spanish and Vietnamese, the two main languages other than English spoken in the neighborhood. They distributed these in the neighborhood with an announcement about the upcoming harvest festival. In the meantime, Professor Heather called the PTA garden coordinator, and together they arranged for the community college students to host a trilingual nutrition information booth at the harvest festival. On the day of the event, over a dozen immigrant families attended and visited the booth.

Teachable moments become learning opportunities when the foundations of classroom and community are forged together as reciprocal collaborations. To that end, community-campus enriching collaborations must be characterized by open communication, inclusive participation, shared decision making, constructive feedback, and principled problem solving (terms identified by actual community partner representatives). Faculty, students, and community partners alike must commit themselves to being adaptable, flexible, and communicative, because individuals and organizations are full of inconsistencies, and life itself brings unexpected complexities but also lucid moments of insight.

College Student: "At first I was very frustrated because my GED mentee came late or didn't show at all. I wanted to stop coming—if she didn't care, why should I? So I complained to the agency director, who encouraged me to ask a few questions to get to know her. I learned that she was a single mom with young children who worked part-time and took care of her disabled mother. I learned just how much she did want to complete her GED, and it completely changed

> my perspective. I realized that
> our time together was so valu-
> able to her even if she couldn't
> make it each week. I spent time
> planning the tutoring if I had to
> wait for her to make sure that
> we made the most of every
> moment."

Individual and organizational reciprocal relationships do not arise spontane-
ously overnight. Rather, they are the result of organic growth of personal investment
and conscientious partnership building across weeks, semesters, and years. Thus,
it is important to understand the progressive nature of establishing and nurturing
collaborations.

To illustrate this concept, Campus Compact (see Torres, 2000) has explicated the following eight benchmarks for each of three stages in developing reciprocal community-campus relationships: designing the partnership, building the
collaborative relationship, and sustaining the partnership (see Table 3.1).

What is notable about these three stages is that the responsibility is shared
mutually across campus and community; each carries the load of accountability for
attending to overarching goals and logistical details. The designing, building, and
sustaining of the relationship relies on conjoined energy that is informed by feedback,
evaluation, and iteration. In other words, enriching collaborations are dependent on
the consistent quality of interactions.

TABLE 3.1
Benchmarks for the Stages of Reciprocal Community–Campus Relationships

Stage 1: Designing the partnership	• Founded on shared vision and clearly articulated values • Beneficial to both organizations
Stage 2: Building the collaborative relationship	• Composed of interpersonal relationships based on trust and mutual respect • Multidimensional: participation of multiple sectors that act in the service of a complex problem • Clearly organized and led with dynamism
Stage 3: Sustaining the partnership	• Integrated into the mission and support systems of the partnering organizations • Sustained by a "partnering process" for communication, decision making, and the initiation of change • Evaluated with a focus on both methods and outcomes

> **Community Partner**: "The college students provided direct service to at-risk school kids, the homeless, and the elderly, but they also served as the *glue* between the college and the community, helping to form alliances across the various non-profit organizations."

Fundamentally, the notion of reciprocity highlights the characteristic and context distinctions between the concepts of **charity** and those of **solidarity**. Service performed based on the notion of charity assumes a "savior" mentality, where privileged college students come to "save" the community from their own "self-inflicted evils." Such interactions are likely to denigrate community members, perpetuate stereotypes, and reinforce systemic power inequities that prevent individuals and populations from progressing (Mitchell, 2008). Robert Lupton (2012) termed this form of service "toxic charity." He argued that the good intentions, passion, and hard work of those "providing" service are not enough to prevent the demoralization of individuals and communities of those "receiving" service.

Indeed, Baker-Boosamra, Guevara, and Balfour (2006) asserted, "Educators must address the pitfalls of privilege that often go unexamined in relationships between groups of affluent university students and the underprivileged populations that service-learning programs traditionally seek to serve" (p. 479). In short, *helping should not hurt* by reinforcing inequities and disparities across individuals and organizations.

In contrast, engaging students in service as a form of solidarity seeks social justice through collaborative empowerment of individuals and communities. By its very nature, solidarity requires common purpose and shared process, articulated and acted on by all participants (Heldman, 2011).

- *Charity:* College students majoring in chemistry travel to an inner-city neighborhood school that is plagued by gang violence to organize and facilitate an after-school science fair for middle school students. They plan and advertise the event and evaluate the science projects.
- *Solidarity:* College students majoring in chemistry travel to an inner-city neighborhood that is plagued by gang violence where they team collaboratively with middle school students, their siblings, and parents to conduct an after-school science fair. Older siblings are recruited as tutors to assist with the science project development, and parents serve as judges the night of the event. Faculty provide college students with research and readings on the relationships among poverty, education level, and juvenile delinquency, about which they discuss and write reflection papers.

Engagement with the community as a form of solidarity echoes Freire's (2000) advocation of educational empowerment for community gain. Those who have been traditionally oppressed will reform and elevate their positions not through handouts from others but instead by "joining hands together."

> **Lila Watson, Aboriginal Activist and Educator:** "If you have come here to help me, you are wasting your time.
> But if you have come because your liberation is bound up with mine, then let us work together."

Contemporary scholars (Avila, 2010) have emphasized the significance of **critical reciprocity** in campus-community relationships in order for meaningful and sustainable change to occur, whether centered in the individual or in the collective. If systems, processes, and practices are not critically evaluated and deconstructed, then replication of existing inequities will remain unchanged.

Critical reciprocity starts from the premise that campus-community partnerships should be conscious of organizational inequities and privilege, strive to be power neutral, and realize mutual benefits within the context of long-term relationships. Of course, critical reciprocity may be a utopian notion given societal hierarchies and injustices (Pompa, 2002).

Still, as a form of critical service-learning (Butin, 2005; Mitchell, 2008; Rhoads, 1998; Rice & Pollack, 2000; Rosenberger, 2000), community capacity building and impact are dependent on reciprocal campus-community partnerships characterized by mutually defined goals, activities, accountability, and solidarity (Cress, Burack, et al., 2010).

Case Example: The art department at an elite college in Boston wanted to create a service-learning course. One of the faculty was on the board of an organization that served at-risk youth and approached the executive director about the possibility of collaborating. The executive director was interested but cautious, unsure of how an art program would benefit his youth and somewhat nervous about the interactions between the mostly middle- and upper-class college students and the impoverished youth with whom he worked. After initial discussions, the faculty member and director mutually decided to "test the waters" before fully immersing themselves and their organizations.

The executive director arranged for the faculty member and two students to meet with a group of youth to explore common interests. The youth were most interested in a mural project, and although they were open to working with college students, they wanted to retain some control over the project. Ultimately, a youth advisory council was created to work with the college students on location, design, and implementation of a mural in their shared neighborhood.

The mural project was a success, building trust between the youth advisory council and the college students. So much so that the youth expressed a desire to share their experiences with others, which the students arranged with the college's media department to turn into a film project. On Martin Luther King Jr. Day, the youth and students organized a community dialogue on race and social class in their neighborhood. Today, this partnership between the college and the agency includes service-learning courses in economics and urban planning that are working to address systemic issues of urban poverty that impact youth.

The principles of critical reciprocity are powerful when thoughtfully enacted. As a further example, community representatives who partnered with colleges through a California Campus Compact program described the nature of their relationships with higher education institutions as **communally beneficial**. The agency directors used such terms to describe their campus colleagues as "committed to social justice"; "passionate for process and outcomes"; "consistent in communication—both listening to and sharing perspectives"; "patient, adaptable, and flexible"; and "utilized their intelligence for inclusion rather than exclusion." In addition, the community partners stated emphatically that as a result of the service and service-learning activities, their organizational capacity exponentially increased to meet community needs, thereby directly contributing to social and economic vitality.

Thus, the first step for community partners in efforts to **ESTABLISH Relationships** with a campus administrator, faculty, or student is to ask, *How might this collaboration be* **mutually beneficial***?*

Ask: How might this collaboration be mutually beneficial?

- Can the college provide enough student volunteers to assist with homework completion for high school sophomores at the Boys and Girls Club?
- Can the community partner provide tutor effectiveness training for the student volunteers assisting at the Boys and Girls Club?
- Will the students commit to and actually provide tutoring for 3 hours each week from September 15 to December 15?
- Will the community partner supervise and evaluate college student performance by providing critical feedback and guidance on tutoring skills?

Assuming that there are mutually adequate and satisfactory responses between community partners and the college representatives, the next question could be, *How might this relationship be sustained over time in the spirit and realization of* **solidarity** *and* **reciprocity***?*

Ask: How might this relationship be sustained over time in the spirit and realization of solidarity and reciprocity?

- Can the college commit to soliciting student volunteers each semester?
- Can the community partner commit to training and supervision each semester?

- Will the college explore other strategic connections such as involving education faculty in evaluating the effectiveness of the tutoring assistance on learning outcomes, high school achievement, and future aspirations of college volunteers?
- Will the community partner share its grant-writing expertise with, for example, the Ethiopian Student Club and collaborate on a grant application for support services for immigrants and refugees?
- Can both the community partner and the college representative agree to act within the context of critical reciprocity that is characterized by open communication, honest feedback, and mutual adaptability?

> "We work with over 40 schools and colleges. The differences in relationship and outcomes are dependent upon commitment, clarity, and follow-through."

> "When faculty or college staff are overwhelmed and don't stay connected to their students, then the result is often detrimental to the success of our programs."

> "Many of our staff are college service-learner alumni. The relationships span multiple generations of faculty and students who passionately committed themselves to serving and learning across differences of affluence and race."

As we discussed in chapter 2, there are multiple possibilities for collaborating with campus offices, centers, and courses. But after the initial contact or introductory e-mail, ask, *How can a community partner facilitate discussions and agreements characteristic of enriching collaborations?*

These conversations will be the most fruitful if community partners use language and ask questions framed not just by logistics (*what* can happen) but rather by approaching such communication as co-educators who articulate *why* and *how* such collaborations need to be undergirded by the values and principles of reciprocity. Ultimately, as the community partner co-educator, you are conveying the *context* and *characteristics* that will define an enriching collaboration.

Crossing Cultural Boundaries

As we discussed in chapter 2, colleges are usually divided organizationally into *academic affairs*, *student affairs*, and *business affairs*. Implicit within each of these units are the primary values that drive operations: Academic affairs is concerned with curricular learning; student affairs is concerned with personal growth; and business affairs is concerned with fiscal efficiency. Therefore, being cognizant of the terminology and language that you use with representatives (faculty, staff, students) from these sectors will increase the likelihood that they understand your agency. In essence, these are not just organizational categories that you are crossing but rather *cultural boundaries* that are framed by implicit values and principles.

Often, we think of culture as related only to ethnic, racial, or religious differences between groups of people. Indeed, historical traditions, experiences, and backgrounds tend to separate individuals in their understanding of one another's culture. And, as we unfortunately know, extreme reactions to these differences can have dire outcomes. We will immerse ourselves in these aspects of cultural boundaries in later chapters in offering strategies for building bridges across cultural divides of misunderstanding in the context of community service experiences with college administrators, faculty, and students. But culture is an inherent and key component of any organization, and missing (or not being aware of) the cultural clues that give meaning and purpose to individual actions and organizational procedures can frustrate and undermine developing collaborations and relationships.

Case Example: Karin is the volunteer coordinator at an organization focused on youth involvement in democracy. At her nonprofit, an energetic and creative atmosphere pervades the work environment. The staff enthusiastically share ideas and change course in their plans if doing so would be more appealing to the high school audience they target. Music is often heard playing in the office, and program leaders can be seen charismatically rallying groups of young people to conduct voter registration drives or attend political rallies.

This high-energy and youthful environment led Professor Martin to believe that the organization would be an ideal partner for his advanced political science class. Together, he and Karin discussed college students serving as "democracy tutors" for the high school kids, researching initiative issues on the fall ballot and working together to increase voter awareness and participation in the community.

Unfortunately, the collaboration did not go as planned. The fast-changing environment of the nonprofit, which worked well for the high school kids, led to several last-minute date changes for the college students—most of whom were juggling work obligations along with school and needed to schedule their time in advance. One day the college students showed up at the organization for a tutoring session, only to find no one there. They later learned that the youth were at a city council meeting, and the organizers had neglected to tell anyone at the college that the session would be canceled.

Even though the college students could envision how being demo-cratic tutors could be beneficial for youth, they were frustrated about what seemed to them a "lack of organization and communication." Furthermore, they were concerned that their grades, which were based in part on this service-learning experience, would be nega-tively affected. In turn, the agency staff and high school youth felt that the college students were too "inflexible," and their need for planning was counter to the "go with the flow" approach of the non-profit. Ultimately this partnership did not end well, with sour feel-ings on both sides as a result of different organizational cultures and expectations.

To explain further, Wilber (1999) depicted organizations as having both external and internal dimensions that fuel the motivations and drive the behavior of indi-viduals in those organizations. The external (or explicit) dimensions are the processes and practices that make the organization operate. These are usually relatively easy to understand and can be seen in actions, behaviors, and policies. For example, at a college, the *external dimensions* are procedures like how students are admitted to the institution or how they register for a course.

More important, however, are the internal (or implicit) dimensions of the insti-tution. The *implicit dimensions* are the tenets of belief and philosophies from which spring the explicit dimensions (see Figure 3.1). These are usually quite difficult to understand and are primarily unseen principles. For instance, if an institution, like a community college, values open academic access to all learners (the implicit prin-ciples), then how students are admitted (the explicit processes) is probably a simple formality of completing an application form. In contrast, if an institution values the enrollment of "high-achieving" students only, then the application process is prob-ably rather complicated and competitive.

Most people do not walk around pondering the implicit dimensions (values) of the organization. Instead, they make decisions and act on what they think makes sense to them and their office, program, students, or clients. But these behaviors are significantly influenced by the culture of the organization, because most individuals try to align their actions so that they are consistent with the goals of the group.

For example, if college students see agency staff at a service site participating in the games *with* middle school students, then the college students are likely to emulate this behavior and play with the middle school students too. Clearly, the *explicit behavior* is to interact with middle school students because the *implicit values* are the importance of developing interpersonal relationships with youth. Alterna-tively, if college students see agency staff directing and organizing games (such as in the role of a coach), then college students will model this behavior and facilitate

Figure 3.1.   Hidden (implicit) and observable (explicit) organizational dimensions.

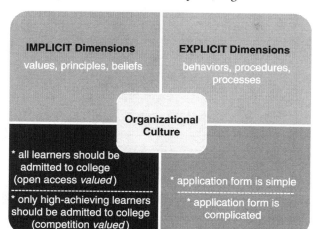

the activities. In this scenario, the *explicit behavior* is to direct and organize middle school students because the *implicit values* are safe spaces for group cooperation and interaction.

In these scenarios, either set of implicit values and either set of explicit behaviors are appropriate. It all depends on the organization's goals and processes for reaching those goals. The problem, according to Wilbur (1999), is that frequently when individuals or groups initiate or develop new processes or activities (like new community service experiences or service-learning courses), the focus on the *what* (the explicit actions) may not relate well with the *why* (the implicit principles). Wilbur cautioned that such efforts are likely to lack sustainability over time if there is not an explicit connection between actions and attitudes.

Creating *collaborations of excellence* that are bonded in *reciprocal solidarity* is an outgrowth of core values, and the implications of this are clearly defined in terms of individual and organizational actions. There are various strategies for doing this that we will further explicate in chapter 4 and chapter 5, but one technique for community partner co-educators to utilize is the *service-learning educational matrix* (see Figure 3.2).

This service-learning educational matrix can function as a heuristic device for visualizing connections between internal values and external actions across organizational units.

Use the
service-learning
educational
matrix

- How is the mission statement of your agency realized through your programs?
- How are the outcomes of a campus program or course facilitated through learning experiences?
- How can common values of the two organizations lead to serving and learning activities?

Although your initial reaction may be that using this kind of diagram to help frame discussions for establishing relationships may feel forced and even "hokey," it

Figure 3.2. Service-learning educational matrix.

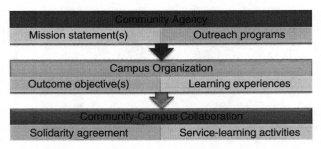

ensures that core values and principles are articulated from the outset. This activity is key, because the evolving nature of programs, courses, and activities will change, and it is practically guaranteed that misunderstandings, challenges, and dilemmas will arise. To progress from *initial* explorations to *building* the collaboration to *sustaining* a relationship on a long-term basis, experiences and expectations may need to adapt relative to the common agreement. Indeed, the original solidarity agreement may need to be revisited over time. But this provides a clear starting point for conversations for reworking external structures and logistics.

These kinds of discussions may also prompt articulation of common agreements for legal and liabilities issues associated with the collaboration. Unfortunately, many institutions (and campus individuals) have been so worried about liability issues that they are reluctant to engage in serving and learning for fear of potential costs if something goes wrong. Such fears have maintained the divide between campuses and communities, depriving students and communities of the mutual benefits of engaged learning.

But, as Richard Cone (2002) asserted, college and university administrators must accept the challenge to work through the details of liability issues as evidence of institutional commitment to good citizenship and engaged pedagogy. Cone admonished institutions slow to integrate community-based learning by questioning the *societal price of inaction*. He wrote,

> What is the cost to society of children not learning to read when a little tutorial help from a college student would provide the little boost that many of them need? What is the cost to society when a free clinic has to limit the number of patients it can accept because there are no volunteers helping with patient intake? (Cone, 2002, p. vi)

Although no liability agreement can replace quality experiences and structured programs or courses, which are the first line of defense in protecting students, clients, and organizations, serving and learning safely is dependent on a clear understanding of risks and liabilities within the context of campus and community opportunities. Of course, all these factors should be premised on strong reciprocal partnerships because risk is best minimized through forethought and preparation. Although most colleges will have policies, forms, and contracts specific to their own institution, we provide next a number of terms and elements of common agreements between campuses and agencies with which to familiarize yourself as you navigate the legal realm of such collaborations and formalize commitments to the relationship.

Common Agreements

As you establish relationships with campus personnel, you may encounter questions about liability, responsibility, or other legal precautions. Like any organization, colleges and universities seek to protect their students' safety and themselves from legal claims. In fact, many colleges employ risk managers and have legal counsel on staff to help facilitate and negotiate the myriad contracts involved in operating a campus. In so doing, institutions usually create guidelines for the community engagement of their students, faculty, and staff and for community use of campus facilities and resources, including off-site locations.

Similarly, at most community agencies, contracts, background checks, and other legal agreements are standard procedure. However, unfamiliar procedures may feel like cumbersome barriers to collaboration. Considering what might be asked of you as a community partner and your own agency's legal procedures ahead of time can smooth the way for dealing with these issues when they arise.

Chapter 4 and chapter 5 will explore additional individual rights and responsibilities such as understanding pro bono work for serving on an agency advisory board or agreeing to abide by drug and alcohol policies. As well, we will discuss not just legal issues in these chapters but also ethical dilemmas and issues that may arise in engagement activities. Next, however, we provide common organizational procedures and agreements for protecting learning and serving experiences that may require formal documentation and signatures.

Background, Fingerprinting, and Reference Checks

Perhaps the most common form of legal precaution is the background check. Community organizations that work with vulnerable clients or otherwise enlist volunteers to help with sensitive material or personnel typically have their own procedures for background checks. Some cover the cost as part of the expense of doing business, whereas others ask volunteers to pay for the screening, and still others defer to a central office (such as a school district administration building) to handle background checks.

Students may not be expecting to have to pay for their own background checks and could scoff at the expense; even if they are attending a college with a high tuition, they do not necessarily have a lot of money to spare. If you encounter students who are unable to pay for their background checks, it might be worth a call to the campus office of service-learning to see whether they or another department might be able to cover the cost—especially if the student is taking a required course. (One campus in Seattle, Washington, was able to secure an external funder to pay for all student background checks!)

Ask about covering cost of background checks

The turnaround time for background checks should also be discussed with students and faculty so that they can plan accordingly. In some cases, a community agency may not routinely conduct background checks, but the college may deem that one is necessary in order to protect the institution from a claim of negligence.

> *Case Example:* At a liberal arts college in a small town, the local school district discontinued background checks because of the expense and paperwork hassle. When that college's attorney learned of this change, she advocated for all students volunteering at the schools to have checks conducted through the college, to be sure that the institution had undertaken proper measures of precaution. However, given the cost and time associated with background checks, the campus office of service-learning did not have the capacity to conduct background checks for students involved with the school district. Today, students are still volunteering, most without background checks.

This kind of situation can lead to tense on-campus and off-campus relationships if there is not a shared understanding of *who should take responsibility* for background checks—perhaps a case for discussion among upper-level administrators at both organizations.

As well, it needs to be determined *who is responsible for interpreting* the results of background checks. For example, if an organization that deals with children requires a background check and it turns out that the student has a DUI, who decides whether to accept or reject that student? Specifically, if this information is not relevant to the student's work (e.g., he or she is not driving as a service-learning task), then can the student still engage in the community service?

An additional point to consider with background checks is international student volunteers. Many campuses are increasing their enrollment of international students, who are often in the same classes as American citizens, with the same obligations for service-learning. Because international students don't have a Social Security number or residential history in the United States, though, background check procedures are a moot point.

It may be worth investigating what kind of screening international students have had in order to get a student visa; some agencies consider the visa alone to be indication of sufficient screening to serve. If a student visa is not enough, then community agencies may need to consider whether alternative forms of screening (such as an interview) and modifying service tasks are viable options.

Memoranda of Understanding

Besides background checks, another legal issue that may arise in campus-community collaborations is whether a *memorandum of understanding* (MOU)—also referred to as a *memorandum of agreement* or MOA—is needed. An MOU is a legal agreement that establishes shared understanding and outlines the responsibilities of both parties, including such details as the duration of a partnership or project, any financial obligations, release of liabilities, and consequences for reneging on the arrangement (such as a nonrefundable membership fee). Although often used for long-term and complex partnerships, especially those involving international relationships, MOUs are also employed for one-day service projects or weeklong intensive service experiences. An MOU may also be developed if a community group wants to use campus facilities, such as a branch of Special Olympics using the college gymnasium.

> *Case Example:* Pacific University has a long-standing partnership with the Navajo Nation and small community of Lukachukai, Arizona. Every January a group of students and an instructor travel from Oregon to Arizona to tutor children and chop wood for the elders, as well as to engage in a deep cultural exchange. The students stay at the Lukachukai charter school's boarding house, for which the university pays a usage fee. An MOU between Pacific and the Lukachukai school board spells out issues of liability, cost, timing, and responsibility.

As you delve into the early stages of collaboration, **inquire from the beginning about whether an MOU will be necessary**. Few things temper the good intentions of a partnership faster than having a heap of paperwork on a short timeline because the legal details were not discussed in advance. In a recent case involving an immersive service experience during spring break (e.g., alternative spring break), a project involving students traveling from Kansas to Mississippi to work on wetlands restoration was canceled because the community partner did not have enough time to process the MOU document with the central agency office for approval before the project was to start. Likewise, on campus an MOU may need to be reviewed or signed by the attorney or an administrator, which can delay engagement.

Ask whether an MOU is necessary

Knowing what is required by your agency and what the collaborating campus will require is essential to confirm before the project unfolds. In some cases, umbrella insurance, general liability insurance, accident and injury insurance, worker's compensation insurance, vehicle insurance, and medical insurance are just a few of the items that need to be stipulated as part of the MOU or MOA.

Know the requirements

One volunteer coordinator from a city parks and recreation office recommended that the college she was working with develop the MOU and liability forms because she knew that getting something through her city's legal office would take too much time, and she was not permitted to enter into agreements on the city's behalf.

If working through your own internal bureaucracy will take several weeks, or if you do not have authority to enter into an agreement with another entity and will need to seek upper-administrative approval, be clear on these points from the beginning. Some organizations have such well-developed release of liability forms that simply sharing those with campus partners during the project development phase is enough to reassure college legal counsel.

Ask the college to develop the MOU if you need to

Film and Photography Release Waivers

Documentation may be needed for photography or filming of serving and learning either on behalf of your organization or clients or on behalf of the college students. You may, in fact, need to be explicit with students and faculty about photography or video recording. Imagine, for instance, that John is a student from a college in your town. He has been a coach in your youth recreation program for the semester as part of an exercise science class. He has to give a presentation at the end of the term and figured he would simply snap some photos of the kids at the next soccer game to show his project in action. Would he need to gather photo release forms from youth participants? From their parents? What if his instructor wanted to pass along the images to the college public relations office to put on the website? What if your organization wanted the photos to include in your annual report?

Social Media Usage

In this age of social media, having clear agreements through discussion or legal documents about appropriate sharing of material and contact information is necessary. Students might unthinkingly "friend" a younger mentee on Facebook, for example, which is not in and of itself a legal problem but could become one in certain circumstances. Discuss these issues at an institutional level with the campus office of service-learning or civic engagement to help to establish a strong organizational partnership, and discuss them again with students to reinforce policies (see chapter 5).

AmeriCorps Members

Another instance in which legal issues may arise is with AmeriCorps and other service corps members. Whether they are situated within a community organization or on campus, AmeriCorps members have a specific position description and professional expectations, including activities from which they are prohibited from engaging in. Ironically, these prohibited activities may even be types of service performed (such as tutoring), if the focus of the position is directed toward specific issues such as health care or disaster relief.

Sometimes college campuses and community organizations apply together for a shared AmeriCorps position, in which case the AmeriCorps agreement involves three parties: the college, the community organization, and the AmeriCorps granting agency. If that is your situation, review the contract carefully to ensure that your agency's expectations for service will be met. In addition, the contract may stipulate that AmeriCorps members collect data for their reporting requirements (see also chapter 6). Clarify from the outset the methods and types of data to be collected.

Student Roles and Responsibilities

Although these issues will be explored more fully in chapter 5, consider whether specific student activities need to be delineated in an MOU or MOA. For example, will students utilize agency vehicles to transport clients? If so, will students' driving history be reviewed? Will students have access to confidential information or computer records? If so, must they complete an online confidentiality certificate course before such access is granted? Will students be serving food or potentially come into contact with bodily fluids? If so, must students be cleared for hepatitis?

Each campus with which you partner is likely to have widely varying policies and procedures related to legal issues and sometimes approaches are inconsistent within the same college. Although many people find paperwork irritating and "legalese" difficult to decipher, the underlying purpose of addressing legal issues is nevertheless important: to protect all parties and ensure that when accidents or incidents happen—and they do happen—that the organizations can proceed with the collaboration intact, even if the legal team gets involved.

Furthermore, be aware that negotiating these agreements may bring you into contact with campus personnel other than your primary partners. You may find yourself in discussion with a campus attorney or an administrator in charge of partnerships who has authority to sign legal documents. Sometimes when a financial matter is involved, such as a fee a university is paying to stay at your facility during an alternative spring break, the vice president of finance or the chief operations officer may be involved. When in doubt, ask your primary contact for help understanding who is responsible on campus: It's easy for those within the campus walls to forget that others may not be familiar with their system.

In sum, plan ahead for common legal and liability agreements. Advocating for yourself as a co-educator means that you have considered the risks, protections, and opportunities for your own program or organization. If necessary, check with your organization's legal authorities before reaching out to campus partners. And when campus partners reach out to you, be sure to include your organization's legal needs in the unfolding process of establishing and formalizing relationships. Indeed, if your campus liaison doesn't mention anything about legal issues, then it is up to you to raise the issue! Your college counterpart might not realize that there is paperwork to consider if he or she has not had to deal with these issues before. Most of all, though, don't let the legal work bog you down. It has to be done, and for good reason, but it's one small piece of what goes into outstanding collaborations.

Plan ahead for common legal and liability agreements

Conclusion

Enriching collaborations are established and developed within the context of reciprocal relationships and characterized by beneficial outcomes for community and campus alike. To realize this ideal, however, colleges and organizations need to make an investment of time and thoughtful conversation, have an environment of trust and open dialogue, and have a recognition of cultural and power differences among organizations and individuals. And although a legal agreement cannot dictate reciprocity, it can establish responsibilities and instigate discussions about the logistical details that could otherwise create barriers to reciprocity. The next chapter suggests how you as a co-educator can *engage faculty* in reciprocal and enriching collaborations.

4

ENGAGE FACULTY

Overview: This chapter explains the various conflicting *roles of faculty work life* that may complicate their ability or willingness to engage in a co-educational collaboration. To help community partners overcome such organizational impediments, we offer them an array of co-educational strategies and methods that they might suggest to faculty to engage them in teaching, research, and service activities that align with their professional interests and responsibilities in order to create mutually *enriching collaborations*.

- Comprehending Faculty Work Life
- Communicate Co-Educational Goals
- Create Objectives and Expectations
- Co-Construct Content, Assignments, Activities, and Timelines
- Compare Experiences for Improvement

"To serve is beautiful, but only if it is done with joy and a whole heart and a free mind."

—Pearl S. Buck

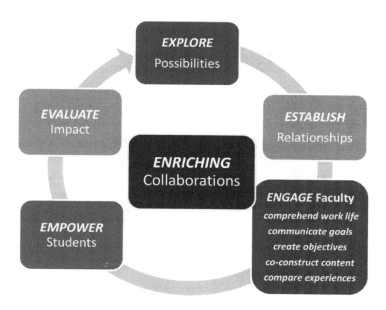

Comprehending Faculty Work Life

College teaching has historically focused on the life of the mind: the types of knowledge that students learn through interactions with faculty, classmates, and academic content. In fact, the concept of a "liberal arts" college education is based on the notion that students must be taught how to "liberalize" or "free" their minds from traditional ways of thinking. As one frees one's mind from simplistic paradigms, then, supposedly, one can think critically and creatively in solving problems and applying innovative ideas.

Thus, the purpose of college education is to make "great thinkers" from which it is assumed will emerge "great leaders" to helm our communities, cities, and nations. Even today, the two premiere student learning goals contained within nearly every college mission statement are critical thinking and leadership.

But as we have learned the past few decades, knowledge alone is not enough to solve local and global challenges, and it does not necessarily facilitate insightful and effective leadership. Yes, the world needs smart people, but it needs smart people with compassion, cultural competence, and communication skills. To that end, colleges have come to realize that integrated learning and leadership development is best facilitated in context and application. Thus, service-learning has emerged as a potent pedagogical approach.

> "The world needs smart people, but it needs smart people with compassion, cultural competence, and communication skills."

Still, many faculty may not know how to initiate community-based learning collaborations, or they may have experienced unsuccessful attempts in the past, or they may be looking for ways to improve their learning and serving components. Here is your opportunity to become a co-educator by helping college faculty figure out the steps and strategies for facilitating students' knowledge and skill development! The point is to **engage** faculty in your efforts.

Naturally, this assumes that you want to be involved with a service-learning or community-based learning course. Certainly, just hosting volunteers from a student club or working with an administrator from a student affairs office, such as residence life, may be more to your liking and comfort level (for more contacts and office ideas, refer to chapter 2). But the fact is, as a community agency professional, you have expertise and associated knowledge and skills from which students can learn critical thinking, leadership, intercultural competence, and many others. Indeed, your expertise in these areas may surpass that of faculty! So, forming a reciprocal co-educational relationship with an instructor may be the best environment for shaping students' learning and growth. But where and how do you begin to work with faculty?

Get recommendations from your colleagues

As we highlighted earlier, start by getting recommendations from colleagues regarding interested or willing faculty. (Note that we use the term *faculty* to generally denote instructor, lecturer, professor, or anyone teaching a college course.) Or contact the office of civic engagement or center for academic learning to see if it can suggest possible faculty collaborators. Last but not least, search the websites of colleges to view faculty course listings and areas of research and scholarship. Many faculty have web profiles containing their curriculum vitae (otherwise known as a résumé) with descriptions of their scholarly agendas (what they research) and links to their published books and articles.

A great icebreaker with faculty is to comment on an idea that you may have gleaned from one of their recent articles or presentations. From there, you may be able to engage in conversation about how these ideas connect with the work you do in the community.

Link your work to the faculty's scholarship

Just like you, college instructors are very busy and pulled in many different directions in their jobs. College faculty not only teach their courses but usually have to advise students about courses and careers, serve on institutional curriculum and policy committees, and are expected to publish and present their research (depending on their institution) and secure grants.

Thus, comprehending the multiple dimensions of faculty work life can be an important step in identifying how best to engage instructors as co-educators. As we suggested earlier in this guide, knowing the language, terminology, and lingo of academe can help you navigate its hallways and personnel. As well, understanding the implicit values and explicit operating principles can help inform your own decision making about whether and how to commit to collaborations.

> "We have worked with Professor Gordon for 4 years and have mutually improved the course and our client service effectiveness. He used some of the data to publish a book chapter, and now we are writing a grant together."

Although variations exist across types of colleges, there are three main areas of faculty work life: teaching, scholarship, and service (see Figure 4.1).

Figure 4.1.   Dimensions of faculty work life.

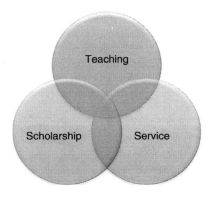

The first dimension, teaching, is usually defined as some form of student instruction regardless of location, because teaching can happen in a classroom, online, in a laboratory, in an art studio, or in a river valley. Credits for courses are usually associated with the number of student contact hours that occur over an academic quarter, semester, or term.

Ask how many hours are required

- Ask early on how many service hours or service assignments are expected in the course and what role these play as part of the course credit. If this is a three-credit class and the faculty wants to add an extensive service-learning aspect, perhaps the course should increase in credits, or maybe students can register for additional credit.
- Faculty who teach on the quarter system, 11 weeks, may have high expectations that don't meet your own timelines. Even a semester-term course, 16 weeks, may not be enough time to accomplish your goals or realize a worthwhile outcome given the amount of investment you may have to make to train or supervise students. Ask a faculty member if it is possible to have students work with you across more than one academic term. And clarify expectations with them for student service across holiday or other academic term breaks.

The number of courses faculty teach depends on their contract; a part-time or adjunct faculty member may be paid per course, whereas a full-time faculty member may be paid a salary. The type of institution also determines the number of courses expected of a full-time faculty. For instance, at a 2-year community college, faculty may teach three to five courses per academic term because they are not expected to conduct research and publish. In contrast, at a 4-year research university, faculty may teach one to three courses per academic term because they are expected to write and publish, give conference presentations, and obtain grants, otherwise known as scholarship.

Scholarship, the second dimension, consists, in general, of writing articles and books, giving presentations at conferences, exhibiting artwork or giving performances (such as in music and dance), conducting consulting work, and acquiring grants. Usually, faculty have a scholarly specialization area (or scholarly agenda). As highlighted previously, some colleges emphasize teaching, so faculty may have little expectation or pressure to publish. At other colleges, there may be strict expectations of one to three publications per year plus conference presentations and a set amount of grant dollars that must be obtained. This is often referred to as a college culture of "publish or perish"; faculty will not advance professionally and can even be laid off if they do not meet scholarly expectations.

Faculty who are on the tenure track have the most pressure to prove their "scholarly worth." This is because tenure (permanent employment) is granted only to those faculty who clearly demonstrate strong academic accomplishments over a 6-year probationary period. During this 6-year trial period, they are ranked as *assistant professor*, and if they are successful in being granted tenure, they are promoted to *associate professor.* Later, generally after another 4 to 5 years, they may apply for promotion to *full professor* (usually just called *professor*).

- If you are in doubt about a faculty member's degree, title, or full- or part-time status or how to address a faculty member (e.g., Dr. Brown, Instructor Brown, Robert Brown), you are always safe with simply using "Professor" as a catchall title.

You can always call an instructor "Professor"

The third dimension of faculty work life, service, encompasses student advising, committee work, and administrative work. Usually, service refers to the campus, but there can also be service expectations to the larger discipline or profession such as serving on journal editorial review boards and holding offices in professional associations such as the American Psychological Association or the American Chemical Society.

Importantly, rarely is this third faculty work life dimension construed as service to the broader community. Although faculty may list volunteer work on their curriculum vitae or include being on a community agency advisory board, community service is usually thought of as service to the college or the academic field. Thus, there may be confusion and misunderstanding by college colleagues when faculty speak about involving themselves in community service and service-learning with community agencies.

Ideally, faculty try to merge and blend their time and energies across the three work life dimensions. The burden of their teaching, scholarly, and service "loads" can be lessened slightly if there are natural connections among ideas, people, and activities. For example, a faculty member may want to conduct research at your service site and then use these data to write and publish about how his or her teaching methods evolved as a result of a service-learning collaboration.

As a matter of fact, increasing numbers of colleges are encouraging faculty to engage in community-based research. This may be an opportunity for your organization to utilize faculty and student resources to assist with impact and evaluation of clients or services (see also chapter 6), although you may find yourself with an overeager faculty member who doesn't understand your multiple responsibilities and time constraints. As a co-educator, create parameters for the collaboration that work for you.

- Try to identify in advance how your community site, issues, resources, or assets may be able to engage faculty (and their students) in extensions of or new forms of their teaching, scholarship, or service. Offer possible ideas for community-based research, data collection, grant writing, and publication outlets. This is another important component to **critical reciprocity** and **solidarity** (discussed in chapter 3). You are positioning yourself in solidarity with faculty as a co-educator to help advance their professional development and achievement. In effect, this enriches and enhances faculty, students, and communities.

Position yourself in solidarity with faculty

Indeed, the *scholarship of engagement* has become significant for faculty not only in North America but also at colleges around the world. In the United States, the Carnegie Foundation for the Advancement of Teaching (www.carnegiefoundation. org) has been a primary force in higher education to promote college teacher effectiveness in the scholarship of teaching, learning, discovery, application, and community engagement. Although the website is primarily directed toward faculty, you might peruse it to get ideas about how to form research, publication, and grant-writing collaborations.

> *Case Example:* Assistant Professor Hernandez was hesitant about becoming involved with the children's book bank. She is a sociologist, not an English literature scholar. Plus, her department chair had strongly encouraged her to focus on publications and forgo community involvement activities. But she agreed to allow the children's community resource director to speak for 10 minutes in her course, "The Sociology of Families."
>
> Dr. Hernandez learned, along with her students, that the children's book bank (in addition to providing free books for kids and supporting literacy efforts) served as entrée for low-income and immigrant families to get connected with other community resources such as the food bank, low-cost housing placement, and free legal support. She allowed students to earn extra credit that term by volunteering at the book bank, and then she worked with the resource director to revise her class into a service-learning course that integrates course content on family social dynamics and socioeconomic issues with direct service to children and families.
>
> To date, Dr. Hernandez has taught the course four times over 3 years, working with the director to make iterative improvements to the assignments and service engagement activities. Many of her students have continued to volunteer at the site after the course, and one sociology graduate secured a position as the children's outreach coordinator. Dr. Hernandez, in collaboration with the director, is now developing an upper-division capstone course that will involve assessment of community resource projects. And the two colleagues have submitted a joint proposal to the American Sociological Association national conference to highlight student learning outcomes and community impact associated with their campus-community collaboration.

Assistant professors who are on the tenure track, like Dr. Hernandez, are discovering how to most effectively teach their discipline's academic concepts while identifying opportunities for scholarly accomplishment. Although academic theories and research are probably not what get people out of bed every morning, most faculty chose their professorial role because that is what drives their passion and energies. So the challenge for you is to *enlighten* faculty about how their theories, concepts, and research have great applicability in the community—indeed at your own agency or community site! Your task, then, is to *engage* faculty interests by communicating about how collaborating with you will enrich, enhance, and advance student learning and, potentially, their own scholarship.

Communicate Co-Educational Goals

Many faculty and instructors labor under the teaching assumption that "content is king." Certainly, in professional disciplines and fields that have licensing and credentialing requirements (such as nursing, teaching, or engineering), making sure that students have the appropriate content knowledge is critical. Consequently, some faculty may fear that service activities will take time away from student learning and water down their curriculum.

> "Service-learning hones the life of the mind and how we mind our lives."

However, as every faculty well knows, students easily forget facts. True learning is not memorizing that which can be merely recalled; true learning happens in context and when applied appropriately. As well, most faculty have come to realize that with the current information age and the plethora of material on the Internet that learning is more than conveying knowledge. Educated students must make judicious decisions about the relevance and applicability of information. Thus, college students must not only pass the test but also pass the tests of life. To that end, the power of service-learning is that it hones the life of the mind and how we mind our lives.

In other words, service-learning helps to enhance the development and coalescence of the knowledge, skills, and behaviors that characterize educated individuals and allow them to be effective workers, family members, neighbors, citizens, and global companions. Quintessentially, this is the epitome of critical thinking and leadership that most colleges strive to teach. Now, how can a faculty member argue with that logic?

One researcher, Daniel Goleman (1995), termed this kind of overall development associated with the linkage of cognitive, affective, and behavioral realms as "emotional intelligence." In contrast to academic intelligence that is knowing a lot about "stuff," emotional intelligence is knowing a lot about how people, places, and things interact. Studies have proved, after all, that success in life is about knowing how to act, make decisions, and interact in appropriate context.

Not to be confused with the academic disciplines of anthropology, psychology, or urban studies, emotional intelligence matters more than technical expertise and more than IQ because it synchronizes together the mind and heart in recognizing and regulating emotions in ourselves that affect decision making and behavior. Thus, emotional intelligence is the driver of critical thinking, effective leadership, and behavioral outcomes (Goleman, 2004). Service-learning conjoins these realms into emotional intelligence (see Figure 4.2) because students are using their head, heart, and hands.

So, are we suggesting that you e-mail or phone faculty members to tell them that working with your organization through service-learning will improve their students' emotional intelligence? Well, perhaps not exactly. But faculty usually are concerned with promoting students' intelligence as a form of academic content comprehension, critical thinking, and decision making. These particular learning goals and objectives are most readily found in the course syllabus (the written course outline containing the assignments).

Review the class syllabus

- If possible, review the class syllabus (often available on a department website), paying special attention to the course description and learning objectives. Identify how service or engagement at your agency will help promote achievement of the learning goals. What is it about the activities, tasks, or projects at your site that can help students comprehend, understand, learn, develop, expand, articulate, or gain greater academic competence?

Create Objectives and Expectations

In an ideal world, faculty would *engage you* in the creation of their syllabus. But frankly, this rarely, if ever, happens, even in the best long-term reciprocal relationships. Syllabi are technically considered a form of "intellectual property," and most faculty are reluctant (some even openly resistant) to have their syllabi reviewed or revised by others.

Don't critique the syllabus

- Never critique a faculty member's syllabus. Although you might thoughtfully request a copy to better understand his or her academic objectives and approach, don't be surprised if there is hesitancy or if the faculty "forgets" to send it. Your best approach might be to ask a student to share a copy with you.

Figure 4.2. Service-learning facilitates emotional intelligence.

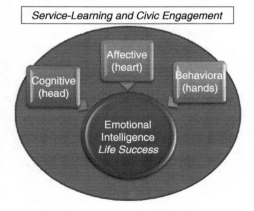

There are online resources you can review for examples of service-learning syllabi. For instance, Campus Compact (www.compact.org) has resources for faculty that contain syllabi across disciplines and institutional types. Also, the Community College National Center for Community Engagement (www.mesacc.edu/other/engagement) has syllabi examples and other resources for faculty and co-educators.

Look at other service-learning syllabi

Most faculty were never taught how to write learning objectives and tend to base the ones they do develop on their own educational experiences as a student or borrow them from colleagues. And even those faculty with service-learning experience don't tend to include service objectives. Hence, here is your chance to offer one to three objectives especially for the service component of the course.

A useful source for developing a service-related learning objective is referred to as "Bloom's taxonomy." A few decades ago, Bloom, Englehart, Furst, Hill, and Krathwohl (1956) developed a list of verbs that progress from the relatively simple to the relatively complex across three human development domains: cognitive, affective, and psychomotor. These are sometimes referred to as knowing/head, feeling/heart, and doing/hands, respectively.

The goal of Bloom's taxonomy is to focus on holistic student development across the three domains by sequentially building from basic knowledge and skills to higher forms of thinking and acting (see Figure 4.3; see also Anderson & Krathwohl, 2001).

At the basic *knowledge* level (first level), learning objectives are measurable and demonstrable, such as list, identify, or record. The taxonomy of verbs then advances to *comprehension* (e.g., describe, discuss, explain), *application* (e.g., demonstrate, illustrate), and *analysis* (e.g., compare, contrast, examine). The final levels are *evaluation* (e.g., appraise, judge, evaluate) and *creation* (e.g., construct, create, formulate). (For a complete description of Bloom's taxonomy and associated verbs, see www.celt.iastate.edu/teaching/RevisedBlooms1.html.)

As a strategy for writing a learning objective, start by identifying the level of knowledge or skill that you would like students to develop as an outcome of the

Start with your goal

Figure 4.3.   Developmental levels of knowledge and skills (adapted from Bloom, Englehart, Furst, Hill, & Krathwohl, 1956).

service activities, tasks, or projects. Recognize that students with little prior community engagement experience are probably not capable of the highest dimensions. As well, younger or less mature students may need more basic levels of support to achieve advancement to the next level.

Indeed, cognitive psychologists like Perry (1970) and social constructivists like Vygotsky (1978) have emphasized the sequential nature of human development. People need multiple experiences and opportunities for reflection in order to develop. In sum, individuals are not capable of instantly advancing to the highest forms of critical thinking and interpersonal interactions. The brain needs time to grow the appropriate synapses.

Use Bloom's taxonomy to create service-learning objectives

Therefore, articulate service and service-learning objectives that appropriately progress throughout the academic term in order to best facilitate enhancement of student knowledge and skills. For example, some general service-learning objectives based on Bloom's taxonomy that you could modify, adapt, and specify to your organization are as follows:

- *Identify* and *describe* the needs of the community population (knowledge level)
- *Explain* the role of the community agency in addressing needs (comprehension level)
- *Model* professional learning behavior to youth and clients (application level)
- *Analyze* economic, political, and social factors contributing to the issues (analysis level)
- *Reflect* on the effect of the service experience on the development of your knowledge, skills, and attitudes (evaluation level)
- *Recommend* leverage points for creating systemic change in the community (creation level)

Certainly, learning objectives are closely related to *expectations of performance*. Essentially, the objectives are intended to articulate that as an outcome of the expected service engagement, these types of learning outcomes will result. As such, clarify with faculty about service expectations and get these detailed on the syllabus. Perhaps, you can even **get yourself invited as a guest lecturer** for 15 to 30 minutes where you can outline the mission and purpose of your organization, the needs and assets of your clients, and the types of service students can perform. Doing so would further underscore your role as a co-educator.

In sum, for optimal service-learning the learning objectives should align with course content, service activities, and reflection assignments. Students' learning and skill development are increased when they understand *why* they are doing it!

Co-Construct Content, Assignments, Activities, and Timelines

Perhaps the concept of *co-construction* is overstated in this section title, because it is doubtful that faculty will sit down with you to solicit your ideas to develop the course. Still, as an expert in your field (and probably as an expert in orientation, training, and evaluation of staff and volunteers), you have a breadth of knowledge that can increase the learning capacity of students (and advance the professional development of faculty).

As we discussed at the outset of the chapter, most colleges and their faculty are concerned not only with teaching academic content but also with developing their students as current and future leaders—in their professions and in their communities. A conceptual model for leadership development that is applicable to all fields and disciplines (and frequently used in service-learning courses) is the social change model of leadership development (Astin & Astin, 1996).

In contrast to traditional definitions of leadership that focus on hierarchical and individualistic notions, the social change model of leadership development emphasizes leadership as change agency that is realized through active collaboration with others toward common purposes. There are three interdependent and dynamic spheres in the social change model—individual, group, and community—and each of these spheres of leadership development interactively informs the others (see Figure 4.4).

That is, *individual* students impact the *group* dynamic and process, and that dynamic and process affects each *individual*; the *group* process works in concert to effect positive change in the *community*, which in turn affects the *group*; and each *individual* connects with the service activity in the *community* and is then shaped by that direct experience as well.

Embedded in each of these spheres are values, attitudes, and principles that drive decision making, behavior, and action. These are known as the "seven Cs" and include *consciousness of self, congruence, commitment, collaboration, common purpose, controversy with civility*, and *citizenship* (see Table 4.1).

As described previously, how individuals practice these values within their sphere of influence both enhance and are enhanced by how individuals practice the values

Figure 4.4. Social change model of leadership development.

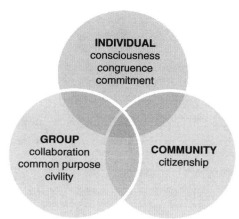

TABLE 4.1
The Seven Cs of the Social Change Model of Leadership Development

Individual Values
Consciousness of self: Awareness of one's own values and beliefs that motivate action
Congruence: Integrity and consistency of one's thoughts and beliefs with actions toward others
Commitment: Passion and intensity to maintain energy in acting congruently toward and with others

Group Values
Collaboration: Working with others in mutual understanding on a shared effort
Common purpose: Performing collaborative work through shared aims and values with others
Controversy with civility: Respectful disagreement that allows for the continued productivity and creativity of individuals and the group

Societal and Community Values
Citizenship: Interconnectedness of individual and group to society at large to create change on a broader level

in the other leadership spheres. The values and principles stimulate and reinforce development of skills across individual, group, and community leadership.

In the social change model of leadership development, as leaders establish their own values and begin to act with integrity and commitment to one or more causes, they interact with small and large groups that can both challenge and reinforce their values and commitments. Through collaboration and individuals' and groups' experience of having a common purpose with others, the concept of citizenship connects individuals and groups to social action that affects change on a larger community scale.

Many college centers of service-learning and student development offices have adopted the social change model to frame their activities. However, this model may be new to most faculty, because it comes from the academic discipline of educational leadership. As such, this is an opportunity for you as a co-educator to engage faculty with a conceptual model in aligning class objectives and activities for broader student learning outcomes.

Apply
the social
change
model

For example, you could work collaboratively with faculty to create a reflective activity that helps students develop *consciousness of self* as they identify beliefs, attitudes, and knowledge about the concepts of volunteering, service-learning, community change, or citizenship. *Collaboration* and *common purpose* could come to the forefront if your community outreach or service project involves working together on a ballot measure or electoral campaign. *Controversy with civility* may emerge in a class discussion about the underlying causes of homelessness, poverty, hunger, or lack of health care access. And, obviously, the point of getting your organization or agency connected to the college is so that students better understand their roles, responsibilities, and opportunities as *citizens.*

By nurturing student growth in leadership, community partners can have a tremendous influence on shaping students' perspectives, knowledge, and skills about how they can emerge from college ready to take action in a meaningful and competent

> "Never doubt that a small group of thoughtful, committed citizens can change the world. Indeed, it's the only thing that ever has." — Margaret Mead (Lutkehaus, 2008)

way on an array of issues. Therefore, we encourage you as a co-educator to involve yourself as much as possible in the co-creation of a service-learning course by suggesting (thoughtfully) to faculty what elements from your own expertise areas may enhance the effectiveness of *learning through serving.* The following list includes a number of ideas to consider:

Suggest materials and assignments

- *Content:* Are there articles, essays, or research from your profession that could be included in the course syllabus to provide students with history, background, or context about issues or client populations? What about websites? YouTube videos? Links to your agency's website?
- *Assignments:* What would best prepare students for serving and engaging at your organization and with your clients? If not recommended readings, research, or annual reports from your organization, what about testimonials from previous volunteer or service-learning students? Or client testimonials?

  o Are there individual skills (like mentoring or coaching) that students need to learn in advance of coming to your site? Are there group processing skills (like program planning or project coordination) that faculty can facilitate before they recommend new outreach activities or complete an assessment of organizational assets?

  o Are there specialized skills in technology or statistics that your organization needs? Are students teaching computer skills to clients? Redesigning your website? Or preparing a community survey?

  o What about intercultural communication competence? Do students have the appropriate knowledge and background understanding to effectively work with your clients and communities? Could you conduct an in-class activity to increase cultural sensitivity and preparedness?

  o Do you have examples or ideas for reflection questions—either ones that students can discuss in class or ones that students can write about? (For more ideas on reflection activities, see chapter 5.)

  o How about final papers? PowerPoint presentations? Websites? Or other alternate ways to demonstrate student learning?

    — If possible, suggest to a faculty member a service-learning objective and an associated activity that facilitates or evaluates student learning or

Suggest a
service-learning
objective
and related
assignments
or activities to
demonstrate it

growth. If the faculty can see the connection and relevance, hopefully so will students. Perhaps offer two to four learning objectives with assignments or activities that support and demonstrate student knowledge and skill enhancement. That way, faculty members may have to use at least one in their course.

– Solicit ideas from current or former student volunteers at your organization. What do they wish they had known before serving? What materials, information, and training were helpful? And what suggestions do they have for faculty in improving the learning and serving experience?

• *Activities and timelines:* Obviously, the most important activity that students will complete is their service at your organization. If possible, the roles, tasks, hours, and timelines should be negotiated and defined in advance with the faculty so that the service component is an integrated learning component of the course while aligned with learning outcomes and assignments and your organization's mission and needs.

Develop
a service-
learning
agreement

In fact, whether or not required by faculty, it is a good idea for you and the students to develop a **service-learning agreement** (or contract). Although you may want to create your own template, at a minimum the service-learning agreement should specify the following:

• Student name, contact information
• Academic term, course name, faculty contact information
• Community site, supervisor contact information
• Service hours; service tasks, activities, and projects (primary, secondary, tertiary)
• Service-learning objectives (three to six specific to term; be specific)
• Academic learning objectives (three to six) that can be facilitated at service site
• Professional learning objectives (three to six) that can be facilitated at service site
• Training or special preparation needed at site (who will conduct and when?)
• Feedback, assessment, evaluation of performance (who will conduct and when?)
• Other considerations

If you do develop your own service-learning agreement form, there may be other information or "contractual type" language that you may want (or need) to add; for instance, statements about client confidentiality, required orientation sessions, dress code or smoking policies, expectations regarding timeliness, resources in an emergency, appropriate use of technology, and so on. (For further suggestions see chapter 5.)

Ideally, faculty and community partners work together to create the service-learning experience and adequately prepare students to engage with community members. As well, students may need course readings, research, and reflection activities to help them recognize stereotypes, their own privileges, and the possible power imbalance that exists between them and community members if the students are to engage in effective learning and serving. Faculty members are academic experts, but you are the community expert. Early and ongoing communication with faculty can help ensure a well-designed experience and timely adaptation and revision, if necessary, that promote collaborations of mutual college-community enhancement.

Compare Experiences for Improvement

Case Example: An associate professor in English at a primarily White, 4-year residential college heard about service-learning as a powerful pedagogy for comprehending grammar and increasing literacy when she attended a session at the national conference of the Association of Departments for English. She decided to try a community engagement component in her course the next term by requiring that students complete 20 hours of tutoring service at an urban school of their choosing.

Rather than contacting the school administrators herself, she had students do so the first week of the term. Out of the calls and e-mails to 12 local schools, only two principals agreed to allow the students to offer tutoring. And by midterm the college students complained to the professor that the high school students they tutored were distracted and disrespectful. In fact, one student wrote in her reflective journal, "I don't know why we are here. If the kids don't care and their parents don't care, why should I waste my time. I'm paying money to learn, not volunteer."

The professor also received an e-mail from one of the principals, who stated, "While I appreciate the students' good intentions, it seems they just don't know how to relate to Black Urban youth. I'm not sure how much value there is for the students—yours or mine."

As we discussed in chapter 3, the power and potential of service-learning springs from reciprocal relationships. The mere good intentions of individuals are not enough to facilitate insight, learning, or change—whether individual, organizational, or community. Instructors who send students to community agencies without sufficient partnership planning are, in all honesty, ignorant! At the least, they missed an opportunity to provide students critical life learning. And at the worst, they may have reinforced misconceptions and stereotypes that inhibit cross-cultural and cross-community empowerment.

Ensure faculty engagement

Engaging faculty means holding them accountable not just for preparation but also for continual monitoring and assessment of processes. Look for clear signs of engagement (or disengagement):

- Although they may not be accompanying students to your community site, are they reading and responding to *your* calls and e-mails?
- Are they reading and responding to students' calls and e-mails about the service experience?
- Are they responding to students' reflection activities like web postings, reflection journals, or other papers and assignments?
- Do students mention whether faculty are having in-class or online discussions about the service experience?

As we noted previously, the nature of faculty work life tends to isolate courses and classes as singular instructor enterprises. As such, having a discussion with you, let alone anyone, about what is going well (or not) in the course and service experience may be a novel (and nerve-racking) concept for faculty. It may behoove you, then, to agree in advance with faculty about the specific dates on which you will e-mail, chat on the phone, or have coffee to discuss the service experience. Offering to "compare notes" and "share student feedback" can open doors for deeper examination of service-learning components that may need revision. As well, it may prompt creativity in extending the collaboration in new directions such as research or grant-writing endeavors.

Conclusion

Just like your own work roles, those of faculty are multifaceted. And just like your own work responsibilities, when these can complement each other rather than compete for time and energy, personal and professional efficiency is enriched and enhanced. Effective community-campus collaborations emerge from reciprocal relationships with faculty where your expertise as co-educator is valued and integrated as a part of the curriculum. Creating long-term and sustainable partnerships that effectively address student learning and community needs must engage the professional interests of faculty and community representatives alike. Moreover, frequent feedback and consistent assessment processes should lead to iterative improvement of learning and serving experiences. That is the specific focus of the next chapter—how to evaluate community-campus processes to ensure optimal learning and community impact.

5

EMPOWER STUDENTS

Overview: This chapter looks honestly at the challenges and rewards of working with college students as a form of educational *empowerment*. To be an effective co-educator, you need to embrace the tasks necessary to help students understand your organization and their role in it. This may require you to provide appropriate *cultural preparation* and guidance in *problem-solving dilemmas and controversies* for your students. As well, students' engagement with your organization is an opportunity for mentoring, *career coaching*, and professional skill development, whether it is a long- or short-term experience.

- Cultural Preparation
- Constructive Controversy
- Career and Life Coaching
- Condensed Connections

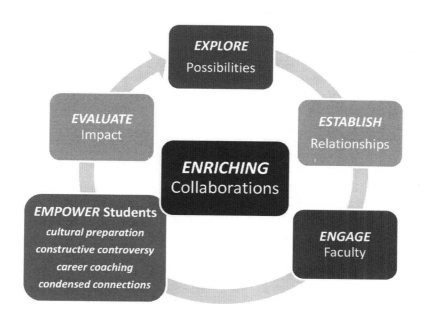

Case Example: Monica was an older-than-average student in a community-based learning general education class at her university. Having taken a break from college for a few years to travel in South America, she had returned to finish her degree and follow her passions for social justice, though she was not entirely sure in what direction her interests would take her. In her class, she was able to provide volunteer service at a shelter for homeless families, where she primarily cared for children in the play center. While serving at the shelter, she got to know the family counselors, program coordinators, and play center staff, as well as the families who came to utilize the shelter's resources.

At first, Monica was shocked by how disorganized the shelter seemed. People were constantly coming and going, the paperwork used on-site seemed like it hadn't been updated in the past decade, and the executive director was always out of the office. The environment was so different from the only other work environment she had ever experienced, her campus work-study position in the financial aid office.

During a biweekly check-in, Monica's supervisor, Sue, asked how everything was going, and though Monica didn't share all she was feeling, she did reveal that the shelter wasn't what she had expected. Sue had seen this reaction before and spent time explaining the organization's source of funding (donations that the executive director sought in meetings outside of the office), how the nature of homelessness led to a constantly changing clientele, and that each of the staff had such a big caseload that no one had time to take on something that seemed simple, such as revising their internal materials.

After the meeting, Monica had a much better understanding of the context of her contribution to the organizational mission and offered to spend some of her time every week revamping the office documents. Excited by the student's initiative, Sue asked Monica to update the handouts and lead orientations for each new group of volunteers. Over time, Monica spoke further with the staff and learned more about homeless counseling and program coordination. As she gained insight into each of these jobs, she decided to declare an academic major in a social work degree and eventually applied to a master's program, for which Sue gave her a fantastic recommendation.

Collaborating with colleges may seem like a great way to boost the people power at your organization, and indeed, a few extra hands can go a long way in resource-thin agencies. However, as this vignette illustrates, as a co-educator in community collaboration, you have the opportunity to shape students' perceptions of your field, help them find ways to excel that are beneficial to you and your clients, and contribute to their professional development and career decision making.

Nurturing students' growth and empowering them to maximize their learning can enhance your experience as a supervisor and deepen your relationship with campus representatives as they see students making connections between academic learning and community service. Of course, fundamental to facilitating an environment of learning and empowerment is adequate preparation of students in terms of the organizational culture, clients, and staff with whom they will work. Although a faculty member or campus administrator may provide some of this preparation for students, you are the resident expert on the issues and opportunities of your community and agency. As a co-educator, offer your knowledge and wisdom as a guest lecturer in the course so students can ask questions of you *before* interacting with clients. Or, as we suggested in chapter 4, provide the instructor of the service-learning course with readings or research that can be integrated into class assignments.

Be a guest lecturer

Helping students achieve their full potential as learners and servers is dependent on well-designed and executed preparation, reflection, and feedback. This chapter presents strategies for *empowering students* and maximizing their community impact across these three educational elements (preparation, reflection, and feedback) and across organizational and community cultural variations.

Cultural Preparation

Organizations

Students are bound to arrive at your agency with varying levels of experience in organizational contexts and with a range of sophistication around issues of diversity and equity. As a co-educator in service-learning, you can play a critical role in what students learn about culture, both in the organizational sense (e.g., how nonprofit agencies and NGOs operate) and in terms of individuals and communities with respect to race, ethnicity, heritage, age, sexual orientation, disability, religion, and other factors. Indeed, providing adequate preparation in these areas may be essential to students' service performance and their own satisfaction in the service-learning experience.

Previous volunteer and work experience do not necessarily equate to understanding of organizational processes. In some cases, students will have already held jobs or volunteered in multiple places. Others may have visited their parents' office or workplace. In still other cases, however, they may have never worked—either paid or unpaid—in any setting, let alone one that is similar to your agency's environment.

Although knowing how to dress, answer the phone, or relate to supervisors or clients may seem like common sense to those of us with years of experience, these behaviors are actually skills we learned through interactions with others over time—and what is considered "appropriate" varies greatly across retail settings, restaurants, factories, offices, and schools. In other words, how we talk, dress, and act is organizationally specific.

Furthermore, though many college students have come of age with the same norms as staff in agency settings, generational differences can also exist between students and the employees of their community organization. Many young people today, for example, use text messaging and social media (e.g., Twitter, Instagram, Facebook) as their primary form of communication and may not realize that such communication is not as common or accepted in the workplace. Consider the following true account as told by one faculty member:

> "Jordan waited after class to speak with his instructor about the problems he was having getting in touch with the supervisor at his volunteer site. Jordan said that he had tried to contact her several times but wasn't getting any response. After asking a few questions, the instructor discovered that Jordan was texting his supervisor—at her desk line. This student genuinely did not realize that texting a supervisor is not usually appropriate or that she wouldn't be able to receive his texts on a landline."

To minimize frustration, contribute to students' professional growth, and ready them for the civic engagement experience at your organization, you can take a few steps ahead of time so that students serving your clients and organization's needs are prepared for the experience.

Conduct a Site Orientation or Training

Conduct a site orientation

One of the best ways to ensure that students are well prepared for the specific context of your organization is to conduct a site orientation or perhaps even a formal training. The structure and content of an orientation or training depend on the resources available at your organization, the number of students involved, the kind of work they will be doing, and the connection between students' work and their classroom assignments and activities.

Case Examples:

- A **food bank** conducts a 15-minute orientation before every volunteer shift. The volunteer coordinator teaches the basics of food safety, explains why protective gloves and hairnets are important, and provides some background information on hunger in the state. The students learn what their task is for the day is and then get to work.

- A **charter school** a few blocks from a college campus holds 2-hour orientations four different times in the first 3 weeks of each semester. Past experience has proved that they will have a regular flow of college student volunteers but that not every student will be able to attend at the same time. The school personnel discuss classroom expectations, emergency procedures, mandatory reporting responsibilities for child abuse or neglect, and dress code. After connecting the college students to specific classrooms, they require students to meet every week with their supervising teacher to discuss their service role in the class.

- An **after-school program** serving youth in a local housing development has an ongoing partnership with the psychology department of a university. Each semester the program manager conducts a guest lecture in the second week of a child development course to prepare students for working with the children. As well, the instructor facilitates a panel with former students who describe their experiences working with the youth. In addition, the college students are assigned a volunteer manual to read as homework.

- A **rape crisis center** requires a 30-hour training before students are permitted to answer the crisis line. In weekly 3-hour sessions over the course of 10 weeks, students learn about sexual assault, legal procedures, how to provide emotional support, how to protect themselves emotionally, the types of mental health problems that callers may have, domestic violence, and community resources. Students must commit to a year of service on the hotline—at least two shifts a month—and go through a screening process in advance of the training.

As demonstrated in these examples, orientations and trainings can be customized for your organization's needs, in combination with the kind of arrangement you have for student service-learners. The extent to which you cover legal matters or the specifics of your clientele will vary depending on your mission and the nature of work students perform with you.

Discuss Policies and Procedures
Just as you would not start a new employee without discussing some basic policies and procedures, the same should be true of working with college students—even if the scope of the discussion varies. Service-learning students might not need to know every detail that is covered in the employee handbook, but a few critical items are good to discuss with anyone who will be part of your organization for more than a single day:

Discuss policies and procedures

- *Emergency procedures:* What happens at your organization in the case of an earthquake, a tornado, or a hurricane? Every region has natural disasters at least once in a while, and students should know details such as evacuation routes and where first aid kits and fire extinguishers are located. Many schools—as well as other organizations—have now implemented active shooter procedures as a result of tragic events around the United States. Anyone regularly in the building should be familiar with safety systems and processes.

- *Inclement weather policy:* How are decisions made at your organization about coming to work in bad weather? Do you follow a local school district? Use a phone tree? Let workers use their own judgment? It is best to discuss the system you use—and include students on any phone trees or broadcast alert systems—before the cause arises. In addition, because students may be tuned in first to their own college's inclement weather policy, it might be worth exploring what to do when your organization and the college have made different decisions with respect to the weather to avoid confusion later.

- *Absences and late arrivals:* If a student must miss his or her service shift, do you prefer to be notified by telephone or e-mail? At what point would you start feeling frustrated or concerned about too many absences? How late is too late for someone to show up to his or her service obligation? In addition to reviewing these kinds of concerns with students, you may need to have a conversation about health and wellness. If you work with a vulnerable population—or just want to avoid getting sick yourself—students may need to be explicitly told not to volunteer while ill. Many students do feel a strong sense of obligation to their service sites and do not want to let down those they are serving. It may be important to explain what the standards are in your agency about calling in sick.

- *Dress code:* What is appropriate attire at your organization? Don't assume that students know what to wear when they come to your site. Although some students will readily adapt their own clothing to serve in an organization (or would not wear anything of concern in the first place), others might need more specific guidance, from footwear to cleavage lines. Even if you do not have a stated dress code in your organization, a conversation about attire may be a valuable contribution to students' professional development and understanding of organizational culture.

- *Prohibited behaviors:* Be sure to review organizational policies with students, even if they seem to be common sense. What is your policy about smoking in or near the building? Drug and alcohol use

> The service-learning coordinator at Eastern State College received an e-mail about a student volunteering at a local senior center. The student's casual attire—extremely short skirts and tops revealing her cleavage—had caused a "horrified" buzz among the elderly residents. The senior center activities coordinator was concerned that the student's attire was interfering with educational and physical therapy programming at the center.

on-site? What about social media use when it comes to posting photos, connecting with clients, or making references to your organization? These kinds of issues should be discussed with students even if you don't have a formal policy about them. Given that for some students, their work with your organization may be the first of its type, considerations such as confidentiality or boundaries simply may be unfamiliar to them, and you have an opportunity to share why these issues are important in your field and the profession.

Indeed, policies and procedures exist for a reason, and it is often helpful when working with college students to explain that reason so that they are learning the rationale along with the rules. There will always be outstanding students who seem to intuitively know what to do and demonstrate leadership in serving your organization. But in alternate situations, students may not know how to act or take too much initiative without checking with staff or adhering to agency protocol. Obviously, this can create problems for clients and staff. Helping students navigate your organizational standards contributes to effective service in the short run and, hopefully, more efficient civic engagement in the long run.

Team Up With Campus Partners

Campus faculty and professionals often recognize the need to provide training or orientation for civic engagement and service-learning students before they embark on their projects. They may offer or require orientations for students working in the community. Whether as part of a service-learning course or a separate workshop offered by an office of civic engagement or career center, there may be an opportunity to address many issues in a broad way that affects multiple partners so that you can focus on the specifics of your organization during an on-site orientation. You might also offer your own input into the content of a campus-based training, or perhaps a service-learning director will ask you to be on a panel of community organizations to provide your perspective. Regardless, finding out what is (or is not) happening on campus can help you know what additional preparation you need to provide to students at your site.

Team up with campus partners

Topics That Provide Preparation for Organizational Culture:

- Dress code
- E-mail etiquette
- Phone etiquette
- Use of photos, pictures, or client information posted to social media
- Issues of confidentiality
- Troubleshooting: what to do when there's a problem or emergency

- Appropriate use of technology, including cell phones
- Attendance and timeliness
- Decision-making processes
- Policies and procedures
- Organizational structure, flowchart

Provide Regular Reflection and Feedback

Provide regular reflection and feedback

What is the best feedback you have ever received from a supervisor about your job performance in terms of learning or professional growth? Were you able to play an active role in evaluating and reflecting on your own strengths and weaknesses? Was the experience simply "top-down"? Or, alternatively, were you encouraged to critically reflect on your performance and identify future learning goals in conjunction with your supervisor?

Civic engagement is an educational experience for students, and one of the cornerstones of learning is receiving feedback about what is correct and incorrect or what could be done better and how. Although a faculty member may provide opportunities for academic reflection, as a co-educator you can offer students further insights into their knowledge, skills, and service performance in order to enhance their overall educational experience.

Even if students are "working for free," if you provide them with the opportunity to reflect on their service and offer feedback on their performance, you can empower them to further their service effectiveness by creating an organizational climate in which tasks are taken seriously and where the contributions of individuals are valued.

- *Meet regularly:* Perhaps you have one student or a few students who will be under your supervision for several months. Scheduling time for regular meetings, either as a group or individually, can pay long-term dividends. Even the most independent of students will likely feel well supported at your organization with weekly or biweekly check-ins during which they can ask questions and review concerns, and you can let them know what has gone well or poorly in their service since the last meeting.
- *Review performance:* Although performance reviews are standard procedure with employees, they are often overlooked with students. Nevertheless, even if a student is with your organization for only a few months, going over what is working and what needs improvement midway through the experience can be mutually constructive. The student has a chance to improve, and your organization can benefit from that improvement, leading to enhanced community impact. In addition, you may also be asked to provide an evaluation of the student's work for an instructor at the end of a term (see Figure 5.1). In such cases, it can be especially helpful to have a set of agreements or expectations from the initial placement arrangement that you can then refer to as part of a more formal review.

Figure 5.1.   Sample service-learning evaluation.

Student performance	Poor	Acceptable	Good	Excellent
Quality of contributions				
Willingness to work				
Cooperative attitude				
Works well with others				
Acceptance of supervision				
Takes initiative				
Courtesy / professionalism				
Personal grooming				
Punctuality & attendance				

As we mentioned in chapter 4, you might suggest to faculty that students create a **service-learning agreement** (or contract). Essential elements in the service-learning agreement are students' learning goals and service tasks to accomplish those goals *that are congruent with your organization's needs*. In other words, students should ideally discuss the learning agreement with you at the outset for mutual acceptance. Then, this agreement can serve as a tool for ongoing performance review.

Suggest a service-learning agreement

Another idea is to conduct an exit interview so that you can learn more from students upon their departure about what you as a supervisor or organization could do differently in the future, if anything.

As a community partner in civic engagement, you might not have the organizational resources or staff capacity to provide each kind of preparation or reflection activity described here. However, you might realize that investing time in training and orienting students to your agency will be worth the reward of working with more productive and capable students. Although students have knowledge and skills to contribute to your clientele, the more you can directly facilitate the development of those skills and offer constructive reflection and feedback, the more likely it is that students' confidence and effectiveness will increase. Helping students connect to your organizational structure, processes, policies, and procedures is the first step in creating an empowering serving and learning experience. The second, and probably most important, step is preparing students for the individuals and cultural communities with whom they will work.

"Other than babysitting, I never had a job, so I didn't know what to expect or what to do. The orientation gave me ideas for how to work with the moms and kids at the shelter. It was scary at the beginning, but then I got to know them, and they saw me as a resource for help. For the first time, I was viewed as a staff member with knowledge and skills. And I was seen as part of

> an organization trying to end
> domestic violence. It's amazing
> to feel part of a larger effort to
> make our community safer."

Communities

In addition to organizational preparation, promoting student empowerment entails appropriate cultural preparation. Students' relationships with the community surrounding the campus will vary from school to school. In some cases, such as an urban community college, students may come from the neighborhoods around campus and be familiar with local demographics. Perhaps students remember an after-school program sponsored by the college from their younger days or have a grandparent who spends time at the senior center that draws many community college student volunteers.

In contrast, a residential liberal arts college that enrolls students from around the country and around the world may introduce to the community students who are newcomers who are not well versed in the local history or culture. As such, students may not realize that a Somali immigrant population has settled a few blocks from campus or understand how the history of the neighborhood has affected the community climate and how their interest in helping and serving is perceived.

Providing students with the cultural preparation to best work with the individuals and particular communities your organization serves is an essential component to empowering their learning and enhancing their success, and it is necessary whether students are from the local community or another part of the region or country. Moreover, this kind of preparation can help prevent embarrassing or offensive incidents that can set back an organization's work or create tensions rather than enriching collaborations. (Recall the situational example from chapter 4 when an instructor sent his primarily White class of students to volunteer at a primarily Black school without calling the principal or checking with the administration in advance.)

As discussed previously regarding organizational preparation, grounding students' knowledge in community cultural dynamics can take place at an agency site visit, a workshop training at your organization, or on campus as part of a class lecture or civic engagement orientation. Regardless of the location, some contexts and issues are particularly important to cover with students.

Appropriate Language and Terminology

Don't
assume
prior
knowledge

Although college is often a time when students develop a critical consciousness and deeper understanding of culturally sensitive and appropriate language, one cannot assume that such knowledge exists prior to a civic engagement experience or that it has covered the particular community groups your organization serves. Furthermore, students may come from an area that lacks a substantial population of a racial or ethnic group that is present in your town, or even the preferred terminology may be different.

For example, whether the ethnic descriptor preferred by individuals or groups is "Hispanic," "Latino," or "Chicano" varies dramatically by region and is usually associated with political, social, and economic contexts. Students might have good intentions, but without specific guidance, they may say something offensive. Community partners can also work with faculty members to cover issues of appropriate language in class. For further illustration, consider the following:

- Is it better to describe your clients as *old people*, *seniors*, or *elders*?
- Do community members prefer to be called *gay* or *queer* rather than *homosexuals*?
- Are the incarcerated juveniles referred to as *delinquents*, *inmates*, or *residents*?
- Should the high school students be called *kids* or *students*?
- Does the community prefer the term *Black* or *African American*?
- Is *homeless* an appropriate identifier, or is *client* or *member* used?

> **Community Partner E-mail to Faculty:** "Could you please discuss with your class why the term 'Orientals' is not appropriate?"

In short, names and identifiers matter. Equip students with the appropriate terms and language for your community (or communities). You might also provide background and historical information about your communities that have functioned to determine local terminology. To draw on the previous example, as you are probably aware, in one community individuals might use the term *Hispanic*, whereas in other communities (or even within the same community) an individual may prefer the term *Latino* or *Chicana* as a self-identifier.

Equip students with appropriate language

Local Historical Context

The history of a community can very much shape how students' work unfolds. Background on government initiatives, new or long-lived racial tensions, controversial events, or even neighborhood landmarks or leaders can provide students with information and perspective that can assist them in their work and client interactions.

For instance, a history class at Kingwood College in Texas (near the city of Houston) investigated a historically segregated African American community in the area called Bordersville. The motivation for the project came from an alarming rate of destruction of many cemeteries. The Bordersville settlement dated back to the 1920s and was long neglected by the greater Houston community, not even receiving running water from the municipality until 1980. Students worked with the Texas Historical Commission to clear brush and restore grave sites. They also interviewed African American elders in the community to help document and preserve life histories in the era of segregation, which included separate schools, hospitals, and baseball team, which played in the Negro League. One student reflected,

> "I was shocked how little most
> people in the area knew about
> Bordersville. We are saving the
> history of this place."

Indeed, history and historical incidents can affect the interpersonal relationships of neighborhoods and communities decades later. Sharing such information and knowledge with students and faculty as a part of cultural preparation can help everyone involved thoughtfully and sensitively plan for effective service and educational efforts. Consider the following case.

> *Case Example:* A group of college students at City University were in a public health class where they had to complete a civic engagement project. The students were working with the county health department to raise awareness about the flu vaccine and were tasked with going door-to-door to distribute brochures and invite residents to a clinic. Time and again, however, they did not get much further than explaining they were university students working with the health department before people would close their doors, without taking the pamphlet.
>
> Unbeknownst to the students, 3 years previously the city had passed a bond measure to fund the expansion of the university, which included purchase and demolition of a church, convenience store, and two houses through city policies known as the "government power of eminent domain." Little did the students know that their new science building had caused tremendous friction in the neighborhood. Though there had been protests and angry community meetings before the bond measure, many residents had given up the fight now that the new buildings were in place. Still, they harbored resentment that a long-standing church had been sacrificed to the university and that it seemed to be forgotten to all but them.

If you were the supervisor at the health department in this scenario, how do you think you could have prepared the students for the potential reaction and resentment that these students were about to encounter?

Power, Privilege, and Stereotypes

As a member of the larger community, you may already have a good sense of how college students are perceived by those around you, including your clients. Are they viewed as active contributors to the community? Elite snobs? Well intentioned but naive? On a "savior" mission?

The dynamics of "town-gown" relationships vary widely by institution, the kinds of students the institution has attracted over the years, and the history of campus-community relationships in a particular locale. Students may be more or less aware of the educational privilege they have as college students, not to mention possible socio-economic or other cultural privileges. They might also be coming to a service project with preconceived notions of why people need help or the causes of social problems.

> **College Student Reflection (following one week of service at an after-school tutoring program):** "If the parents just got involved with their kids' education, we wouldn't have to be here."

Ideally (as we noted in chapter 4), faculty and community partners work together to prepare students to recognize stereotypes, their own privileges, and the possible power imbalance that exists between them and community members. As well, interactions between students and community members can be complicated by layers of economic and social power that are not readily observable or easily categorized into bimodal labels such the "haves" and "have nots." For instance, the college students may be first generation and come from low-income families but provide service to well-educated residents who have a disability and are unable to maintain their own homes.

Your expertise and role as co-educator can add invaluably to what and how a faculty member teaches students in the classroom, and, in some cases, you might even be able to alter the tone and direction of a civic engagement project by providing your input and insight. In fact, your experience and insights can bring a cultural and educational context to the students and the class that a faculty member, even one who lives in the community, probably could not.

Case Example: Sara is the activities coordinator at the Shady Elm Retirement Community. She was contacted by Martin, the service-learning director of a nearby college campus, where students and the instructor of a first-year seminar class had decided they wanted to partner with a senior center for a service-learning project around the holidays. The class had been doing some reading about Alzheimer's disease, issues of depression and isolation among older people, and generational segregation, and they were excited about the idea of making gifts for residents of a nearby facility to show that they cared.

Sara and Martin met to discuss this potential project, and Martin could tell that even though Sara was eager to partner, she had some hesitations about this particular project. Finally, Sara revealed her concern that by having a project in which students made gifts for the elders, they were perhaps solidifying a stereotype that senior citizens are helpless and lonely, when in fact the elders at her facility were quite active in the community and volunteered with local schools and soup kitchens as long as they were physically and mentally able. As well, not all of the seniors were Christian or participated in gift giving in December.

Sara valued the idea of intergenerational connection but suggested instead that the students in the seminar come to the assisted living center for a visit and work together with the senior residents to solicit book donations for children in the local schools. The students would still be meeting their goals of creating connections with the senior generation, but they would also have a chance to get to know them in a different way, and one that might break down stereotypes while building community.

Issues of power, privilege, and stereotypes are by nature complex and sensitive. Sometimes faculty are interested in service-learning precisely because of the potential of this teaching method to expose students to unfamiliar circumstances that challenge their stereotypes, and yet even if that's the case, the instructor may be making assumptions about both the students' backgrounds and the clients they serve.

What's more, when these topics are not fully explored, students' stereotypes can be reinforced—solidified rather than challenged. Community partners and faculty may be able to work together on both preparation and reflection activities that engage students in critical analysis of their experience that leads to deeper understanding and commitment to social justice, rather than a retreat into ignorance. This understanding in turn can lead to improved community impact.

Suggested reading

A resource that might be helpful in exploring and deconstructing prejudice and stereotypes is *Learning Through Serving: A Student Guidebook for Service-Learning and Civic Engagement Across Academic Disciplines and Cultural Communities* (Cress, Collier, & Reitenauer, 2013). The text has scores of individual and group activities that can be adapted to community organizations. Specifically, the exercises examine the knowledge and skills needed for and facilitated by engaging with the community, including issues of collaboration across culture.

Students' Cultural Background and Identity

A final consideration in preparing students to work with communities in the most effective way possible is the background and identity that the students bring when they serve with your organization. Educational institutions are increasingly diverse, and even if it was once the case that college students represented a particular demographic—historically 18- to 22-year-old middle- and upper-class White students—that may no longer be true. Even "traditionally aged" students today tend to represent more ethnic, racial, cultural, socioeconomic, language, and religious groups. You may even encounter students who are going through a process of gender transition or reconstruction. As well, the colleges you work with may draw students from a particular country such as India or Saudi Arabia. Or the campus with which you are collaborating may be primarily populated by nontraditional adult students who are returning to finish a degree.

Furthermore, as we mentioned earlier, local students who come from the community may face additional challenges, such as feeling awkward about serving people they know, disconnected by the educational privilege they now have, or unable to recognize why others have not followed the path that they did. In one case in Portland, Oregon, African American students who returned to their predominately Black neighborhoods to provide service-learning were referred to disparagingly by some community members as "Oreo cookies" (i.e., Black on the outside and White on the inside).

Unfortunately, stereotypes can be held by community members your organization serves. At a West Coast college, with a particularly high percentage of Pacific Islander students, the students have felt unwelcomed and harassed when shopping or eating at restaurants in the small rural town surrounding the school. In another case, a gay male student felt that he needed to "go back in the closet" at his service site because of intolerant comments he heard from their clients about sexual orientation. These kinds of experiences can detract from students' ability to contribute in a productive way to their community, particularly if they are feeling marginalized and excluded from that community.

In short, few assumptions can be made about students' backgrounds and identities. Community partners may find cause to examine their own policies or approach to working with diverse volunteers, just as they are preparing students to work with diverse clients. Addressing these topics can enhance the experience for students and set them up for success in working with a wide range of individuals and communities. (For more strategies on *navigating difference*, *investigating power*, and *unpacking privilege*, see Reitenauer, Cress, and Bennett [2013].)

Suggested
reading

Constructive Controversy

As important as preparing students for the communities they will encounter in civic engagement is, engaging them in the issues your organization addresses provides a unique and powerful opportunity for co-education. The learning potential of civic participation consists of students not only being on-site and performing certain tasks but also engaging in critical reflection and thinking about how their service can contribute to social change and greater equity in communities.

To that end, perhaps you've witnessed a service-learning student awaken to new ideas while involved at your site, or maybe you've experienced a casual lunch hour conversation that evolved into a deeper discussion with a student about your organization's work. Indeed, one of the reasons some community partners give for their willingness to spend time scheduling and supervising college students is this opportunity to help students learn about critical social and environmental topics—and in a way that is often entirely different from what they glean from a textbook or lecture. This is the essence of co-education and enriching collaborations.

Of course, every issue imaginable that community organizations work on entails multiple perspectives, varying ideas about the best way to provide care or create a change, and a range of associated policy issues. And with such perspectives and approaches come conflicts and controversies. It is the nature of individuals and organizations, of which none are exempt. Honestly consider the following for a moment:

- How does your organization vary from what is happening in another agency working on a similar cause?
- How is your work affected by local, state, or federal regulations and the political climate at each of these levels of government?
- Why do your donors support you, or why do you think you have challenges securing donors?
- What are the key controversies in your work?

Depending on their course work, their experience, and their overall understanding of nonprofit and NGO systems and the process of change, college students may or may not ask these kinds of questions directly. But when a first-year student from another state inquires, "Why are there so many homeless people here?" or a junior returning from study abroad says, "Where I lived they didn't have these issues because families really looked out for and cared for each other," you have a window of opportunity—a teachable moment—to enter into a conversation that goes well beyond "How did it go today?"

As we have noted, the democracy in which we live and work is a grand experiment in balancing individual rights with mutual concerns and in negotiating conflicting values with commonly held principles (Cress & Donahue, 2011). Similarly, campus-community service relationships are not utopian adventures but rather fraught with dilemmas for problem solving.

As co-educators, you can provide students with the tools and know-how for negotiating and navigating the mental and psychological landscapes of disagreement and conflict. Indeed, if framed as an instructive opportunity or teachable moment, we can capitalize on controversies and dilemmas as rich educational environments that *empower students* to learn respectfulness for difference, practice listening without judgment, and promulgate their own voice.

Suggested reading

A resource that might be useful for strategies in negotiating controversies is *Democratic Dilemmas of Teaching Service-Learning: Curricular Strategies for Success* (Cress & Donahue, 2011). Although the text is primarily focused on developing and teaching service-learning courses, there are dozens of tips, techniques, and methods for empowering students in their service-learning experiences, especially when they encounter trials and tribulations.

These kinds of controversial conversations can be tricky to facilitate, often come at unplanned moments, and can sometimes unfold in a rather distressing way—especially when the issues are emotionally sensitive or involve topics that are difficult for many of us to discuss, such as race, income inequality, or faith-based values. Seasoned supervisors of service-learning students might feel comfortable tackling a controversial issue, having done so many times before, or a neophyte might be ready to jump in and see what happens. For everyone else, though, knowing how to approach controversy in a constructive manner can be intimidating.

There are excellent resources for learning how to negotiate sensitive and difficult topics, such as *The Challenge of Teaching Controversial Issues* by Claire and Holden (2007) and annual summer institutes that host trainings on conflict management and cross-cultural communication (see the Intercultural Communications Institute, www.intercultural.org). But there are also a wide variety of nonthreatening and fun activities (see Cress, Collier, et al., 2013) that can be incorporated into student orientations or trainings in preparing students for *working through the differences* in perspective (see also chapter 4). For example, look closely at the picture in Figure 5.2. What do you see?

Most people initially see a duck (or bird) and then with time perceive a rabbit (or bunny). With more time and practice, it is easily possible to perceive both at the same time. Student learning in a community partnership is somewhat like this: framing, reframing, and then reframing again as we move through the process. The challenge, however (and where conflict can emerge), is when our image of the world does not agree with how someone else views the world. Metaphorically, we see "ducks" but the person with whom we are interacting sees only "rabbits." We may even be assuming

Figure 5.2.   Rabbit-duck illusion.

Note. Image retrieved from Wikimedia Commons. In the public domain.

that we are discussing the same "animal" without realizing that our perceptions are different. We may have to work hard, over time, and with patience to shift our perceptions rather than be staunchly held to our views. Using activities like this one can empower students to be curious about perspectives and meaning that they never considered before because they couldn't see it!

Create time for reflection

Another strategy for delving into the challenging topics surrounding the issues and causes you work on is to be proactive by deliberately creating time for students to reflect on their service experiences. According to numerous studies about service-learning (Ahmed, Hutter, & Plaut, 2005/2008; Eyler & Giles, 1999), writing about and discussing civic engagement experiences is one factor that leads to enhanced learning. Reflection is the process by which students take in new knowledge and integrate it into their current understanding—sometimes in fact leading to entirely new perspectives. Keen and Hall (2009) found that inclusion of site supervisors in reflection activities adds an important dimension to student learning. You could consider participating in reflection on-site, as well as joining discussions in the classroom.

Reflection On-site

Reflection can take place before, during, or after civic engagement activities. For example, you could ask students what their expectations are or what they know about a certain issue before a service project begins, thereby prompting their thinking and "getting the wheels turning" while they undertake the day's task. During a shift with your organization, you could occasionally ask how the work is going and whether particular questions have come up or, when the setting allows, begin a conversation about the issues at hand. At the end of the session, consider asking students what went well, what did not and why, or whether anything struck them as surprising or particularly interesting. Even these relatively innocuous prompts can open up students' thinking, so that throughout their experience they are thinking about not only what they are doing but also why, as well as the underlying issues connected to their work.

> *Sample Reflection Questions and Prompts:*
>
> - What are some assumptions you think people make about this topic?
> - What was surprising to you about what we did today?
> - What did and did not go well during today's session? Why?
> - How does the way we provide this service differ from that of other organizations you've been a part of?
> - Why do you think this organization needs to exist?
> - I expected community members to be . . . .
> - What have you learned about the community?
> - What impact do you think your work has?
> - What new questions do you have?
> - How do you feel about what you did today?
> - Will you do anything or think anything differently because of your experience today?

Reflection in the Classroom

If you are working with a faculty member and a particular course, another approach is to work directly with him or her to coordinate your reflection efforts (see also chapter 4). In this kind of scenario, you are ideally already aware of what the learning objectives are for the course and have a good working relationship with the instructor. You might work with faculty to attend class on occasion when discussion is taking place or ask whether there are particular questions you could discuss on-site to better prepare the students for the classroom.

In addition, many faculty assign written reflection papers as part of a civic engagement course. With students' permission (which the faculty member could get ahead of time), you might also be able to read reflection papers, which may provide ideas for further analysis and discussion. Imagine being able to follow up on the questions or issues students raise or to say to a student, "I remember reading in your paper that you felt frustrated by how small your actions seem in the grand scheme of things. I want you to know that your work really makes a difference in our organization and here's why."

As we highlighted in chapter 4, there are multiple avenues that promote students' learning and empowerment when you engage in an enriching collaboration with a faculty member. If a faculty member is showing a film or video in class, maybe you could be part of a discussion about how it connects to your work. Or invite yourself as a co-educator as a guest lecturer or community panel member in class, debriefing community issues, challenges, opportunities, and topics.

As a co-educator you can deepen students' learning by strengthening the connections between your work and their academic studies—an enriching process for all involved. Of course, besides planning deliberate opportunities for reflection and learning, creating an atmosphere of open dialogue, questioning, feedback, and improvement throughout your work with students is the environmental framework for *empowerment*. Indeed, *educative empowerment* will directly impact students' effectiveness and lead to enhanced outcomes in your community work. (For more strategies on learning and "making meaning" through reflection, see Collier and Williams [2013].)

Moreover, the reflective feedback that you provide students serves as a mentoring function for students regarding their personal and professional lives. Mentoring is relationship building for empowerment (Collier, 2013). Thus, mentoring is another form of enriching collaborations, because in addition to developing students' knowledge and skills, you may be suggesting to them academic disciplines, degree options, and career possibilities that they never before considered.

Career and Life Coaching

As we have tried to emphasize throughout this text, the *knowledge*, *skills*, and *attitudes* that students are developing as a part of the community engagement experience with your organization is forming *who* they are and will become as professionals, family members, and neighbors; in essence, how they will *behave* and who they will *be* (see Figure 5.3).

Figure 5.3. Facilitating students' behavior, being, and becoming.

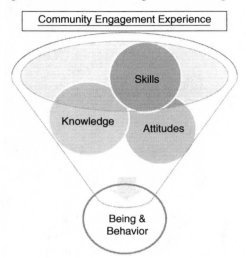

With expertise in your field, you are in an excellent position to provide support and guidance concerning career choices with the students you supervise. Certainly career coaching can include professional development in terms of better understanding organizational culture and processes such as writing a professional e-mail and understanding policies and organizational hierarchies, but life coaching and mentorship can also extend into a domain that many college students find intimidating and perplexing: *what to do with their life*. Civic engagement offers the opportunity for students not only to explore the particular careers relevant to their service placement or project but also to get to know the various paths that the professionals in community organizations have followed to reach their career interests and aspirations.

> **Student Reflection:** "Through my civic engagement project I learned that while I love kids, I'm not cut out to be a teacher."

Although of course some college students have been in the workplace, and many traditional and nontraditional students go to college with a firm career path in mind, for others the "what next?" question is daunting. Furthermore, many students (especially first-generation college students) may lack exposure to the wide variety of career options that exists for them. They may be thinking only of broad categories such as writer, teacher, or psychologist rather than the much more specific grant writer, environmental educator, or youth behavioral specialist.

Case Example: Antoine wandered past the Center for Civic Engagement at his small residential college in Washington State wondering if there was something he could do to get involved with the community. Through discussion with the center's service coordinator, he revealed that he grew up in a low-income neighborhood in California, where he had been involved with a youth program that kept him out of trouble and on track to go to college. The "hook" for him had been spoken word performance art—writing and speaking about what was on his mind in a way that he didn't have the chance to do at his high school. He was hoping that there was now some way that he could give back to the local community by contributing to a spoken word program near the college.

The service coordinator introduced him to Alexandra, the lead teacher at the Community Completion Program—a "last stop" alternative school run by the school district and serving kids who had behavioral or academic challenges and were not successful in the main high school setting. Alexandra immediately saw potential in Antoine and encouraged him to create a spoken word after-school program.

Alexandra suggested that Antoine begin by sharing his story with the teens and then inviting them to join the program. In so doing, Antoine developed greater awareness about his own motivations and values, which he then shared with the youth. He committed to meeting with the youth twice a week—nearly a 2-and-a-half-mile walk each way.

The program was a great success. It started out with a small group of youth participating but grew over time to the point where Antoine needed help to keep it going. He sought the college's service coordinator's assistance to recruit more college students to participate. But with the new student volunteers came differences in opinion about how to operate the program. Fortunately, Alexandra, the lead teacher and Antoine's site supervisor, met with the college students to discuss the challenges of youth programming when well-intentioned volunteers have conflicting perspectives. She facilitated two activities with the college students to help them assess their individual strengths and weaknesses and their group strengths and weaknesses. The efforts served to create new bonds of group cohesion and the decision that Antoine should serve as the group leader because he initiated the program.

Over 3 years, Alexandra continued to supervise and coach the student group through reconciliation of controversies. She also took additional time to mentor Antoine. Specifically, she encouraged him to investigate graduate schools for teaching in the arts, and she served as a reference writer for his application. Antoine was admitted to a top-ranked graduate program on the East Coast.

Introduce
the staff

When you are working with college students, you have the ability to open new academic discipline doors and invite them to consider professional options that they may not have on their career radar. One strategy to help students better understand their career options is to make sure they meet a variety of people at your organization—maybe most of your staff if your organization's size makes doing so realistic. Introducing the staff can be part of an orientation program, or it can be conducted person by person over the course of several months. Ideally, the staff will have a chance to explain not only their job titles but also what they *do*, because knowing that a program manager or development officer exists might not actually help a student understand what these positions entail.

Another approach is to offer students the opportunity to conduct an informational interview—an informal meeting with you or someone else on staff where the student can ask questions about an individual's work roles and responsibilities and learn more about the kinds of knowledge and skills required. Informational interviews are a valuable way of gleaning insider perspective in a safe context, rather than saving questions for an actual job interview or, worse yet, taking a job and then finding out what it really involves, such as completing all the course work in education only to find out later that you really don't have the patience for working with children!

In combination with the reflection and feedback activities that you design for students when considering their knowledge, skills, and service performance, you can create an atmosphere in which students feel comfortable asking career-related questions like, "What do you like most and least about this work?" and "What would it take for someone like me to get hired at a place like this?" Furthermore, informational interviews can also be useful for asking, "What was your major or academic degree?" and "How do you get to where you are today?"

Some students labor under the misperception that they must choose an academic major and career path and that path will dictate what they do for the rest of their lives. There are those for whom this strategy works just fine—they might go to graduate school immediately after completing their bachelor's degree and follow a specific career trajectory, like becoming a social worker, which is completely fulfilling for them. At the other end of the spectrum, of course, are those who take a more winding path toward fulfillment, with a few "false starts" or even enjoyable forays into fields that for whatever reason did not work out for the long haul. Indeed, for many of us, those false starts were not useless but rather provided enriching experiences that eventually led us to our current profession. In fact, the managers at your own organization may prefer to hire employees with divergent job paths if they provide useful perspectives and experiences for serving your clients and community.

Informational interviews, along with casual conversations at lunch or in the workroom, can help students understand these nuances in career trajectories. They may then feel less pressure to pick a particular major or more free to start with something they think they will enjoy and see where it takes them. Of course, the opposite can be true as well. If in your field there is a specific professional path of credentialing progression and it is unlikely that someone will get hired or advance without certain degrees or experiences, then that too is important for students to know and understand.

In your role as a community service supervisor, mentor, and/or career coach, you might also be able to get a sense from talking with a student about his or her specific hopes, fears, interests, and doubts. Asking such questions might lead to an "I don't know" answer, but these questions could also generate a conversation in which students explore possible career directions with you in an unthreatening discussion that can be quite revealing or powerful to them. Perhaps by asking a student what she has enjoyed most or least about her work, for example, you are able to help her see that she enjoys working with high school students much more than younger children, or vice versa. Thus, although career coach may not be a role you considered before as a site supervisor, it can be an enriching collaboration with the chance to make a real difference in the empowerment and decision making of your students—and that may eventually lead them back to your organization as newly minted professionals.

Condensed Connections: Empowering Students During Short-Term Service

This chapter has addressed a variety of ways in which you as a community partner can be a co-educator in the civic engagement experience. Much of the discussion, however, has assumed that you will see students more than once, over an extended period of time such as an academic quarter, semester, or year. In contrast, civic engagement is in fact often brief, limited to a few hours for a service project or perhaps a week or two of intensive work.

What if you are a partnering agency on another continent, and students and faculty are coming for an immersive international experience? Or perhaps you get an e-mail from students at a college across the country who did a Google search on "charities in Philadelphia," and your organization "Catholic Charities" came up. Now they want to do an alternative spring break with you.

Alternative spring break and short-term international service-learning experiences are both growing in popularity at colleges across the United States and around the world. In both cases, a group of students, and often a faculty member or staff chaperone, seek to partner with one or several organizations for an intensive week (sometimes a couple of weeks or even a month) of service-learning. Or what if you are an organization in the same town as a college, and once a year you are asked to host a one-day service project for students?

Empowering students in short-term or intensive civic engagement experiences might be an unlikely prospect and perhaps unrealistic to expect in many circumstances. Nevertheless, with a little adjustment, partners can still co-educate in a way that prepares students culturally and organizationally, that creates opportunities for constructive controversy, and that shares career possibilities. Whether a service project is 3 hours or 3 weeks, community agencies can explore how to maximize time to reach everyone's objectives by communicating well with campus partners.

Even when time is limited, community hosts for civic engagement can ask key questions in the planning process to shape how time is spent. For example, if students found you on Google and are coming from across the country for an alternative spring break, asking what their goals are for the trip and what kind of previous experience they have with the topics or issues will give you a sense of how to balance background information with action.

Make the most of your orientation time

If you have only 15 minutes for orientation as opposed to 3 hours, what you cover will obviously be different, and you may be limited to essential safety and logistical information. Still, during that time you might also be able to plant a seed for a reflection discussion that takes place during a break. Or if you wrap up a few minutes early every day of an alternative spring break, you may be able to open a conversation about the underlying issues of your organization that the students then continue to discuss throughout the evening. Though it may not be worthwhile to introduce everyone on staff, you might be able to chat with students during the course of a day to learn about their career aspirations or share more of your own story.

Furthermore, if students are coming to your organization from abroad or any distance, they might be able to work with you from afar to prepare for the experience. In this age of modern technology, an orientation session via web conference or Skype might suffice in lieu of in-person training. If the trip is part of a credit-bearing course, you may be able to work with the instructor just as you would in your own town to assign reading materials or ask the students to conduct research about the issues your community faces. Many courses utilize an online platform (e.g., Moodle or Blackboard) to host course materials or discussions, even if the course is not fully online. You might able to gain access to the course website to pose questions or provide documents or links before ever meeting the students in person. Again, good communication with college trip planners can help you establish what the options are and to connect with your group ahead of time. (For more information on preparation and processing strategies for global and immersive service-learning, see Cress, Stokamer, Van Cleave, and Edwin [2013].)

Conclusion

As a co-educator in civic engagement, your role is essential to the learning that students experience and also to what they are able to contribute to the community—now and in the future. As you prepare students for service and engage them in the issues of your agency, students will then be better able to make a real impact in the community. Evaluating and assessing that impact is the topic of the next chapter.

6

EVALUATE IMPACT

Overview: This chapter explains how to design and frame evaluation processes in order to optimize the impact of service on student learning and community enhancement. Parsimonious models are explained for simplifying assessment strategies that are theoretically sound and valid. The emphasis is placed on collection, analysis, and dissemination of data for formative assessment, not just summative evaluation, of college and community activities.

- Create Assessment Methods for Impact and Iteration
- Collect and Analyze Meaningful Data for Learning, Enhancement, and Scholarship
- Civic Improvement Through Dissemination and Celebration of Accomplishments

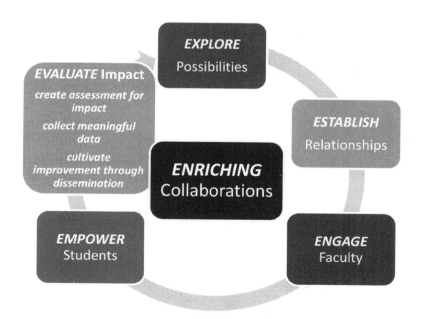

Create Assessment Methods for Impact and Iteration

Evaluation strikes most people as sounding judgmental and critical. Most of us do not want to be critiqued! But the point of evaluating the performance of individuals, organizations, and programs through thoughtful reflection, assessment, and iteration is to optimize the positive transformation of people and communities.

Assessing our ongoing practices means intentionally examining the elements that are functioning well and those that are not functioning well. The purpose of evaluation is like that of a detective—to uncover and discover what facilitates effective service-learning. As such, there are two main types of evaluation: formative assessment and summative assessment.

Formative assessment is best characterized as reflection and feedback in the moment. In other words, utilizing formative assessment techniques means that while we are in the act of service-learning, we are using multiple methods to consciously consider how things are going.

Certainly, one method used by faculty and community partners alike is ongoing reflection activities (e.g., students' written journals, small group discussions), which allows for constant and consistent communication and monitoring of progress among participants. As such, individual and group reflection is a formative evaluation activity that allows us to assess and then adapt, form, and reshape our interactions, behaviors, and practices accordingly in order to ensure effectiveness of service-learning.

In contrast, summative assessment focuses on the end products or outcomes of service-learning. Usually, summative assessment is important for reporting accomplishments to external stakeholders. Often, these are things that can be tallied or counted, like the number of clients served, the number of students who provided service, the amount of new grants received, or the number of new homes built (as in the case of Habitat for Humanity). Being able to point to tangible products or outcomes often assures funders (and ourselves) that progress is happening.

But if the purpose of service-learning is to transform students, colleges, and communities, then formative assessment is more likely to realize this overarching goal. After all, knowing what is going on allows one to modify according to the situation and context. In contrast, if evaluation is performed only at the end, then there is no opportunity to rectify issues or leverage opportunities in the present.

The purpose of assessment, then, should be a *learning cycle* of formative evaluation processes that is inclusive of (a) observing experiences, (b) collecting data or evidence, (c) analyzing the data from which to draw insights, and (d) using those insights to implement strategic actions (see Figure 6.1).

Case Example: At a residential religiously affiliated college, service to the larger community was a primary principle of the institutional mission. Students had multiple co-curricular and curricular opportunities through many different clubs, offices, and courses. But when a new president was hired during a severe budget crisis, she asked the director of the Center for Community Engagement to "prove" that such community service efforts were worth the fiscal investment.

Figure 6.1.   Assessment learning cycle.

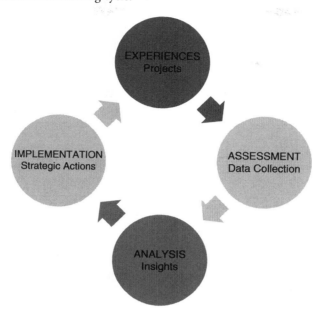

Panicked, he called the Institutional Research Office for help. But the staff there were too busy completing student retention and graduation reports for the new president to offer any assistance. Next, he sent e-mails to three faculty members who were teaching service-learning courses that semester, but after 4 days only one responded, saying that she was overwhelmed grading midterm exams and was not available until next term. Finally, his student worker suggested calling the director of the Boys and Girls Club, their largest community partner.

It turned out that the Boys and Girls Club director had kept data for the past 5 years on the numbers of kids served; the numbers and names of college student volunteers; and the numbers and names of teachers, faculty, and college courses. The director had also worked with a faculty member the previous year to develop an end-of-term survey for college students on academic and social learning outcomes.

Overjoyed at finding these data, the director of the Center for Community Engagement involved the faculty member and Boys and Girls Club director in writing a brief report for the new president, highlighting college and community impacts. They next took their data to the Institutional Research Office, where staff were able to link college student names with retention and graduation rates.

In a very short time, using existing data, the director was able to prove that college students who served at the Boys and Girls Club had increased retention and graduation rates as compared to their peers. In sum, the college investment in these activities was worth it! And, now, they had a collaborative research team that could further investigate why these efforts were working and how to strengthen them even more.

Fundamentally, assessment as learning and iteration is trying to address three primary questions:

- Did our efforts make a difference?
- Why did our efforts make a difference?
- How can we make a bigger difference?

The answer to the first question (Did our efforts make a difference?) is a yes or no response: Yes, our efforts made a difference, or no, our efforts did not make a difference. And to determine whether the answer is yes or no, one can collect either **quantitative data** (things that can be counted), like number of hours learning and serving, number of clients served, or percentage increase of reading scores, or **qualitative data** (how things change, are impacted, or are transformed), such as changes in students' aspirations to earn their degree and graduate. As mentioned previously, usually these summative types of evaluation data are known as outcomes or outcome data.

Certainly, collecting evidence to "prove" service-learning is working is very important. Being able to definitely respond, "Yes, our efforts did make a difference. Students' reading levels improved 31%" is important to programmatic stability and individual motivations for continuing efforts. However, the second question (Why did our efforts make a difference?) is even more critical to investigate and uncover.

Answering the question "Why did our efforts make a difference?" means investigating the antecedents or elements of our success, such as specific teaching strategies, specific service activities, or specific infrastructure or organizational supports that have created the environment for success. Of course, concurrently we are also investigating and trying to determine what may be inhibiting or stifling our success. In a sense, we are trying to discover best and worst practices so that we can alter, revise, amend, or refashion as needed (i.e., formative assessment).

Our findings and insights should, theoretically, allow us to answer the final question (How can we make a bigger difference?). If we did, in fact, make a positive impact, what can we learn to do again (or perhaps do in a slightly varied way) to make an even greater impact? How can we maximize learning? How can we maximize community change? How can we maximize positive impact on individuals, organizations, and communities? This is the iterative process. (*Iteration* means the action or process of repeating a procedure in which repetition of a sequence of operations yields results successively closer to a desired objective. Or, to put it more simply, repeating something to make it better.)

> **Student:** "My service-learning was to work with a classmate and ask neighbors to answer a five-item questionnaire about the assets and strengths of their community. Essentially, my service was a research project. While some people closed their doors on us, others not only answered the questions but were greatly appreciative of the opportunity to think positively about their community. We got into some really interesting discussions and ended up taking notes that we turned into qualitative comments for the report to the neighborhood association board. While the board loved the data, they were most moved by the creative suggestions of neighbors who don't normally come to meetings or share their perspectives on issues."

To address these three big questions (Did our efforts make a difference? Why did our efforts make a difference? How can we make a bigger difference?), we can use some simplified assessment models to help us design an assessment approach and plan that works for colleges and communities.

Collect and Analyze Meaningful Data for Learning, Enhancement, and Scholarship

Formal assessment frameworks and conceptual models can aid us in designing thoughtfully constructed inquiries. There are three methodological models, in particular, that you may find useful in outlining potential assessment projects.

The first is referred to as the **logic model**. The logic model is frequently used by nonprofit foundations and begins with identification of an overarching issue such as "poor health and lack of access to health care." The model realizes that there are multiple contributing factors such as poverty but identifies actionable strategies for addressing the issue in a certain context or community such as through service-learning.

From the service-learning program, specific "doable" outcomes are projected, such as "increasing an individual's knowledge of nutritious foods versus fast foods." Hopefully, this leads to larger impacts such as increased numbers of individuals who eat well. Ultimately, this can lead to healthy communities (see Figure 6.2).

The logic model rationally recognizes that overall community health cannot be immediately, drastically improved. Rather, the approach intentionally operationalizes small, sequential, and achievable steps as a model or method for intervention, assessment, and impact.

Figure 6.2.   Logic model.

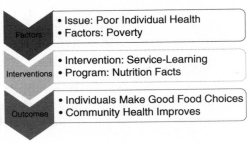

A second assessment and methodological model is known as **Astin's inputs, environments, and outcomes model,** or I-E-O model (Astin, 1993). *Inputs* are defined characteristics that an individual brings, such as one's gender or race/ethnicity. *Environments* are those practices, programs, and processes that have an influence on the input variable. The interactions of inputs and environments then lead to *outputs* or *outcomes* (see Table 6.1).

The idea is to identify key input variables, to specify the interactions of environmental variables (or factors) on the inputs, and to collect outcome data about these interactions in order to convey a clear and concise story. For example:

- *Inputs:* 89% of sophomore high school students
- *Environment:* who participated in the service-learning program to tutor middle school students in math and reading
- *Outcomes:* reported increased likelihood of graduating from high school

A third methodological model or framework for assessing service-learning is known as the **assessment matrix** (Gelmon, Holland, Driscoll, Spring, & Kerrigan, 2001), and its three main components are *concept, indicator,* and *method* (see Table 6.2). The assessment matrix seeks to answer three questions:

TABLE 6.1
Astin's Inputs, Environments, and Outcomes Model: Examples

Inputs	*Environments*	*Outcomes*
I. Student Data	1. S-L Course	A. Increased Learning
II. Client Data	2. Tutoring	B. Increased Reading Levels
III.	3. Projects	C. Improve Access to Nutritious Food
IV.	4.	D.
V.		

TABLE 6.2
Assessment Matrix

Concept	Indicator	Method
I.	1.	A.
	2.	B.
II.	1.	A.
	2.	B.

- What do we want to know? (concept)
- How will we know it? (measurable indicators)
- How will we gather evidence to demonstrate what we know? (methods, sources, timing)

Student example:

- Did students improve their *civic leadership* skills?
  - *Concept:* leadership, civic leadership
  - *Indicators:* knowledge of leadership concepts and skills; ability to identify characteristics of individual and group facilitation strategies; products as evidence of leadership success
  - *Methods:* survey, interviews, focus groups, observations in class and community

Faculty example:

- How does service-learning influence instructor pedagogy?
  - *Concept:* philosophy of teaching, teaching and learning methods
  - *Indicators:* teaching roles, class format, organization, environment
  - *Methods:* observations, interviews, syllabi, survey

Community example:

- What is the civic engagement impact on community partners?
  - *Concept:* capacity to fulfill mission, economic impacts
  - *Indicators:* number of clients, impact on resource and funding utilization, staff changes, program insights
  - *Methods:* focus groups, interviews, document reviews, survey

All these assessment models are ways to outline and diagram an evaluation approach that is meaningful to all participants. As such, the models allow for clarification of assessment goals, definition of concepts to be measured, and identification of the specific populations from which data will be collected.

Establish a baseline of data

Another strategy is to establish a baseline of data at the outset of the project against which you can measure progress. List the baseline information to document the problem. The baseline information should be quantifiable so you can revisit and see your impact at the end of the project. For example:

- Currently, our school has 50 pounds of trash every day and no recycling.
- Currently, the incidence of children at the homeless shelter with dental issues deficiency is 50%.
- Currently, 90% of students at our school think that bullying is a big problem.
- Currently, two senior citizens in the local independent living center know how to use e-mail.

Of course, make sure that any assessment designs are reviewed and approved by the appropriate oversight bodies (such as Institutional Research Boards for Human Subject Protection) on college campuses and that ethics regarding informed consent, waiving participation, anonymity, and confidentiality are ensured for your informants. If in doubt, check with a legal or research expert in your organization or use the resources of the college to confirm the soundness of your assessment processes.

Also, rather than develop new surveys or interview questions, review others that are readily available online for copying. An especially useful resource with multiple assessment tools and instruments is Purdue University Libraries: Service-Learning (http://guides.lib.purdue.edu/content.php?pid=380888&sid=3121307).

Review the research

By perusing research articles (some of which are highlighted in chapters 1 and 2) and familiarizing yourself with surveys, you also gain ideas for concepts of skills, knowledge, and attitudes that can be measured, as well as organizational and institutional levels of understanding that may be important to your internal and external stakeholders (see Table 6.3).

Involve faculty and students in assessment

Finally, as much as possible, involve faculty and college students in your assessment efforts. Although you or your staff may be able to undertake assessment on your own, collaborating with college partners can extend faculty scholarship and increase students' knowledge and skills. Moreover, you will now have more individuals who are, hopefully, in cognitive possession of data about your organization who can articulate to others about your accomplishments in advocating for your organization.

Civic Improvement Through Dissemination and Celebration of Accomplishments

As we noted previously, the purpose and process of assessment is to document evidence and improve efforts to enhance learning and living communities. As such,

TABLE 6.3
Defining Key Concept Indicators for Assessing Development and Impact

Knowledge: I Know	*Skills:* I Can	*Attitudes:* I Value
Client Awareness: I am familiar with the profile of those I seek to assist and understand the issues that contribute to their challenges.	**Adapt Communication:** I can consider the communication styles of those with whom I interact and adapt my dialogue in all discussions and difficult conversations.	**Mission-Driven and Learning Objective Service:** I believe in the educational and change mission of service-learning and commit my efforts accordingly.
Communication and Learning Styles: I understand that individuals have diverse communication and learning style preferences that may affect their actions and reactions.	**Adapt Behavior:** I can consider the behavioral preferences of those with whom I interact and adapt my interpersonal skills in culturally appropriate ways.	**Inclusivity:** I believe that all individuals regardless of differences deserve respect and the opportunity to positively influence their own future and that of the community.
Organizational Structure and Values: I understand the alignment among the organization's policies, procedures, and mission and how I am contributing to effective community service.	**Critically Investigate and Analyze:** I can utilize existing evidence and research alternate forms of data to critically consider antecedents of causes and identify leverage points for systemic change.	**Multiple Perspectives:** I believe that multiple perspectives even when seemingly counter-opposed offer the opportunity for vital and innovative solutions.
Academic-Community Connection: I understand how reciprocal campus-community relationships lead to learning, empowerment, and positive change.	**Creatively Problem Solve:** I can individually and collectively engage in innovative organizational and contextually appropriate improvement methods.	**Engagement as Solidarity:** I believe that common purpose and collective action can empower individuals, organizations, and communities.

disseminating (sharing) your findings and insights allows others to emulate your successes.

Although at the outset this may seem daunting—like developing, collecting, and analyzing a survey—it can also be as easy as displaying a single photo. A picture does tell a thousand words and more. So, you certainly may want and may need to collect statistical data or rich qualitative data that you can integrate into reports for external stakeholders. You might also consider less onerous data for demonstrating impact and disseminating information about achievements, such as the following:

Collect data

- Photo collages
- Videos
- Visual illustrations such as charts and graphs
- Pithy stories, quotes, and short testimonials
- Meaningful numbers: 1 in 4 of the homeless in Oregon are children

Indeed, don't overwhelm yourself with piles of data, numbers, statistics, and tables. If you can't make sense of it, neither will anyone else. If you do create a table, chart, or bar graph, try to keep it easy to read (see Table 6.4).

"We house homeless elders with significant medical and psychiatric issues. Data about incorporating regular exercise into their daily lives was the single most important factor in securing the federal grant to keep us open. The students made an immediate impact on the elders by leading the exercise programs but through their research project have also ensured that future cohorts of elders will be provided healthy living and exercise options."

Sharing data, results, and findings with neutral third-party observers can also challenge your ideas and push you toward deeper insights for enhancing processes and practices. Get students to offer suggestions and recommendations for change and improvement. In addition, your clients may also have helpful opinions and suggestions.

TABLE 6.4

High School Student Responses Before and After the Service-Learning Experience

Question	Before Service-Learning Experience Agreement (%)	After Service-Learning Experience Agreement (%)
I plan to graduate from high school.	68	92
I want to go to college.	31	69
I believe it is important to contribute to the community well-being.	78	98

Last, but not least, students and communities should publicly celebrate accomplishments. Consider a service-learning fair and poster session or recognize students with an award ceremony. Invite families and other members of the public to hear poetry readings, view PowerPoint presentations, or see demonstrations of science knowledge and skills that are outcomes of service-learning projects. In short, share your triumphs.

Conclusion

Thoughtfully constructed assessment is both formative and summative: paying attention to what is happening now so that appropriate adjustments can be made and tracking progress over time to leverage greater impact and garner greater interest in your programs and activities. Rather than feeling lost in a forest of menacing statistics, use the assessment models and frameworks to chart your path and join with others such as faculty and students to help navigate this potentially unknown terrain. And have fun along the way. Fundamentally, assessment is about learning and insight, which should be shared and celebrated.

7

SUMMARY AND CONCLUSION

Excellence in Engagement and Education

Overview: This chapter provides a brief summary of the key issues and major strategies highlighted throughout the book. Whether the civic engagement relationship with your organization is *curricular* (as part of a class) or *extracurricular* (not part of a class but supported by the college), to effectively realize the potential of the *enriching collaborations model for enhancing communities*, each of the model's components (explore possibilities, establish relationships, engage faculty, empower students, evaluate impact) should be continually enacted in ongoing, collaborative, and iterative communication between college and community. The result will be community enrichment and academic excellence in a continuum of co-education.

- Collaborations for Community Enrichment
- Collaborations for Academic Excellence and Engaged Scholarship
- Continuums of Co-Education and Conclusions

Collaborations for Community Enrichment

To achieve critically authentic reciprocity in college-community relationships, community partners must embrace their roles as co-educators in this civic education engagement endeavor. What you know about the community, the skills you have, and what you do matter! As such, your co-educational role contributes directly to students' growth and development because you help students apply what they learn in the classroom to the real world. In turn, both the college campus and the client community are enhanced and enriched.

As demonstrated by the multitude of examples, activities, and case studies throughout this short volume, we have tried to illustrate how to navigate the academic terrain and offered guidance to help you map out your own unique approaches in addressing two fundamental questions:

- **What might be some steps or strategies for achieving a co-educational role?**
- **How can this be accomplished when disparities in power exist between academic institutions and community agencies and the individuals within them?**

Although it is not possible to anticipate every possible encounter, event, or contingency, the strategies recommended here are from actual experiences of community partners and their best practices across years of trial and error in traversing the peaks (highs) and valleys (lows) of civic engagement collaborations. We hope that you have found here a few strategic shortcuts!

Remember, too, that you are not alone on this path. There are countless others and myriad resources to assist you every step of the way, from national organizations such as Campus Compact to college support resources such as campus offices of civic engagement and community-based learning. Despite the fact that the task of working with a college might seem daunting and that it might take you a few times through the process to arrive at a collaboration that is mutually beneficial, *communities are stronger when campuses and community agencies collaborate because it creates knowledgeable and engaged students who give back to their communities as committed citizens long after they graduate.* This is the quintessence of enriching collaborations.

Thus, engaging as a co-educator initially begins with exploring possibilities and establishing relationships with college colleagues (administrators and faculty) and students. The point is to emphasize the skills and knowledge that students will gain from your individual and organizational expertise about community issues, challenges, and opportunities.

Explore Possibilities

Summary:
EXPLORE
Possibilities

- Call on your own professional networks
- Connect with campus centers and clubs
- Collaborate with faculty on community-based research

Establish Relationships

- Convey characteristics of reciprocity based on solidarity (not charity)
- Competently cross cultural boundaries of organizations, groups, and individuals
- Co-design common agreements

In short, you are convincing campus representatives that students cannot achieve development of 21st-century work, leadership, and life skills by merely sitting in a classroom listening to a lecture or blogging online about an academic module. Rather, the enhancement of these cognitive, cross-cultural, and affective intelligence skills require active interpersonal and educational engagement with diverse individuals, communities, and organizations. And you have the site(s) and insight(s) to facilitate these critical outcomes.

Colleges offer opportunities that you might not even have considered. For example, the fact that a certain percentage of federal work-study funds must be spent in the community is a great way to ensure that a student can get paid for working with your organization at no cost to you. A partnership with a college can help with grant funding, as many foundation and government organizations understand that their funds are leveraged when more members of the community are partners. Colleges often have speakers or visiting scholars or guest artists who could be of interest to members of the community and your clients. This is another form of collaboration that benefits all.

Collaborations for Academic Excellence and Engaged Scholarship

Service-learning and community-based learning may be part of curricular or co-curricular programs depending on the college, faculty, students, and staff members involved. It might encompass a semester-long course or a one-day service experience. It might be embedded as a requirement of a professional program (like nursing) or as mandatory service hours for membership in a sorority, fraternity, or student club. Regardless of the academic connection, the ultimate goal is to enhance students' community and civic awareness by providing real-world experience that benefits your organization and the community. As such, whether the activity is "credit bearing" or not, the critical element is engagement for educational improvement—or academic excellence (because this is a phrase that resonates with most administrators and faculty!).

Moreover, in your role as a co-educator, you are providing professional advancement of faculty. For some faculty members, collaborating with a community-based organization is a novel experience, and your expertise in bridging academic and community knowledge will facilitate for faculty new roles as teachers, researchers, and scholars. Ideally, this means building a reciprocal relationship that will endure beyond a single academic term or a specified period of student service-learning.

Engage Faculty

- Communicate co-educational learning goals
- Co-construct learning and serving activities and assignments
- Compare experiences for revision and improvement
- Contemplate community-based research projects for engaged scholarship

In addition, highlight the fact that your organization can serve as a site for community-based research to be undertaken by faculty and students. Increasingly, colleges are stressing the importance of graduate and undergraduate student community-based engagement research. As well, the Association of American Colleges and Universities (AAC&U) promotes the educational efficacy of community-based research as a "high-impact practice," especially as a critical pedagogical practice for helping to increase the academic learning and retention of historically underrepresented student populations, because the technique emphasizes active problem solving through application of knowledge. Furthermore, given the publication pressures that some faculty face in their professorial roles, conducting engaged scholarship in the community helps to coalesce their efforts on and off campus for the betterment of their academic disciplines, college students, and community partners.

Empower Students

- Conduct cultural preparation trainings
- Converse about controversial conversations and civility
- Coach service behaviors, reflective insights, and future career aspirations

Successful collaborations require careful student selection, preparation, and orientation training to ensure that students are adequately equipped to assist the needs of your organization, staff, and clients. As such, keep in mind students' capabilities but also their limitations and liabilities (like we have to tell you!).

In general, students have boundless amounts of energy that can be creatively channeled to help your organization achieve its goals. Many students are extremely skilled in the use of technology and can assist your organization in building or updating your website. And because students are approaching your organization with fresh eyes, they may come up with a novel idea for your major fund-raiser that you might not have considered.

In some cases, students are testing out a possible career path. As a result of the service work that they do with your organization, they might decide not to pursue this particular profession. This should not be an affront to you or your organization. Rather, a student's realization of this fact may actually benefit the long-term enhancement of the community if the student is not suited to this kind of career. As you well know, not all students are cut out to work in nonprofit community-based organizations or education-related fields.

Alternatively, while working with your organization, students may reinforce their thinking that they do want to be a social worker, work with elementary school children, or assist nontraditional students achieve their GED. In short, exposure to what you do not only gives the students a better understanding of what they are learning but also shows them how that knowledge is applied and how they, too, can be part of that experience either by making a particular career choice or by volunteering in their own community throughout their lives.

Evaluate Impact

- Create assessment methods for impact and iteration
- Collect and analyze meaningful data for learning, enhancement, and scholarship
- Civic improvement through dissemination and celebration of accomplishments

Although most agencies and organizations need to collect and report evidence of successful services and impact, framing these assessment efforts as opportunities for strategic leveraging of capacity can shift evaluation from one of critique to one of learning, growth, and dissemination of accomplishments and best practices.

As well, involving undergraduate and graduate students in methodological design, collection, and assessment of data enhances students' knowledge and skills and provides important information for your organization. In addition, faculty interest (and professional need) in community-based research can serve to extend their scholarship and academic discipline. As you are probably well aware, data not only substantiate individual and organizational efforts but also can be the key to securing new forms of funding and support.

Continuums of Co-Education and Conclusions

Enhancing collaborations means that all partners build on their strengths. As the community partner, you have the organizational experience and insight. In turn, faculty provide the course content and academic guidance, and students bring energy and a desire to learn and serve.

As this volume honestly acknowledges, such collaborations are not always easy. It can be a challenge to navigate the jargon of academe, and the structure of a college can be opaque. Even identifying the right person to work with can be difficult, and once that person is identified, he or she might have to jump through institutional hoops to put the program in place.

If there is an admonition here, it is *don't give up!* Putting the partnership into place and managing the trial and error of service-learning may take some time before everyone is satisfied with the process. But what we have learned by working with countless organizations and programs is that ultimately it is well worth the effort.

In conclusion, the bottom line is to communicate definitively what you offer as a co-educator and creatively construct a partnership that enhances the betterment of all. And never underestimate the value of your educational expertise and contribution!

REFERENCES

Ahmed, Z., Hutter, L., & Plaut, J. (2005/2008). *Reflection in higher education service-learning*. Scotts Valley, CA: Learn and Serve America's National Service-Learning Clearinghouse.

Anderson, L. W., & Krathwohl, D. R. (Eds.) (with Airasian, P. W., Cruikshank, K. A., Mayer, R. E., Pintrich, P. R., Raths, J., & Wittrock, M. C.). (2001). *A taxonomy for learning, teaching, and assessing: A revision of Bloom's taxonomy of educational objectives* (Complete edition). New York, NY: Longman.

Association of American Colleges and Universities. (n.d.). *High-impact practices: LEAP campus toolkit*. Retrieved from http://leap.aacu.org/toolkit/high-impact-practices

Astin, A. W. (1993). *What matters in college? Four critical years revisited*. San Francisco, CA: Jossey-Bass.

Astin, A. W., & Astin, H. (1996). *A social change model of leadership development*. Los Angeles, CA: Higher Education Research Institute.

Astin, A. W., Sax, L. J., & Avalos, J. (1999). Long term effects of volunteerism during the undergraduate years. *Review of Higher Education, 22*(2), 187–202.

Avila, M. (with Knoerr, A., Orlando, N., & Castillo, C.). (2010). Community organizing practices in academia: A model and stories of partnership. *Journal of Higher Education Outreach and Engagement, 14*(2), 37–63.

Baker-Boosamra, M., Guevara, J., & Balfour, D. L. (2006). From service to solidarity: Evaluation recommendations for international service-learning. *Journal of Public Affairs Administration, 12*(4), 479–500.

Battistoni, R., Longo, N., & Jayanandhan, S. (2009). Acting locally in a flat world: Global citizenship and the democratic practice of service-learning. *Journal of Higher Education Outreach and Engagement, 13*(2), 89–108.

Bernackiand, M. L., & Jaeger, E. (2008). Exploring the impact of service learning on moral development and moral orientation. *Michigan Journal of Community Service Learning, 14*(2), 5–15.

Bloom, B. S., Englehart, M. D., Furst, E. J., Hill, W. H., & Krathwohl, D. R. (1956). *Taxonomy of educational objectives. Handbook 1: Cognitive domain*. New York, NY: Longmans, Green.

Butin, D. W. (2005). Preface: Disturbing normalizations of service-learning. In D. W. Butin (Ed.), *Service-learning in higher education: Critical issues and directions* (pp. vii–xx). New York, NY: Palgrave Macmillan.

Calmes, J. (2013, May 5). Obama delivers message of optimism to class of '13. *The New York Times*, p. A14.

Claire, H., & Holden, C. (2007). *The challenge of teaching controversial issues*. Sterling, VA: Stylus.

Colby, A., Ehrlich, T., Beaumont, E., & Stephens, J. (2003). *Educating citizens: Preparing America's undergraduates for lives of moral and civic responsibility*. San Francisco, CA: Jossey-Bass.

Collier, P. J. (2013). Mentoring: Relationship building for empowerment. In C. M. Cress, P. J. Collier, & V. L. Reitenauer (Eds.), *Learning through serving: A student guidebook for service-learning and civic engagement across academic disciplines and cultural communities* (pp. 113–121). Sterling, VA: Stylus.

Collier, P. J., & Williams, D. R. (2013). Reflecting in action: The learning-doing relationship. In C. M. Cress, P. J. Collier, & V. L. Reitenauer (Eds.), *Learning through serving: A student guidebook for service-learning and civic engagement across academic disciplines and cultural communities* (pp. 95–111). Sterling, VA: Stylus.

Cone, R. (2002). Preface. In S. A. Joyce & E. K. Ikeda (Eds.), *Serving safely: A risk management resource for college service programs* (pp. vi–vii). San Francisco, CA: California Campus Compact.

Corporation for National and Community Service. (2005). *Martin Luther King Jr. day of service toolkit.* Washington, DC: Author.

Cress, C. M., Burack, C., Giles, D. E., Jr., Elkins, J., & Stevens, M. C. (2010). *A promising connection: Increasing college access and success through civic engagement.* Boston, MA: Campus Compact.

Cress, C. M., Collier, P. J., & Reitenauer, V. L. (2013). *Learning through serving: A student guidebook for service-learning and civic engagement across academic disciplines and cultural communities* (2nd ed.). Sterling, VA: Stylus.

Cress, C. M., & Donahue, D. A. (2011). *Democratic dilemmas of teaching service-learning: Curricular strategies for success.* Sterling, VA: Stylus.

Cress, C. M., Stokamer, S. T., Van Cleave, T. J., & Edwin, C. (2013). Global and immersive service-learning: What you need to know as you go. In C. M. Cress, P. J. Collier, & V. L. Reitenauer (Eds.), *Learning through serving: A student guidebook for service-learning and civic engagement across academic disciplines and cultural communities* (pp. 177–189). Sterling, VA: Stylus.

Cress, C. M., Yamashita, M., Duarte, R., & Burns, H. (2010). A transnational comparison of service-learning as a tool for leadership development. *International Journal of Organizational Analysis, 18*(2), 228–244.

Eyler, J., & Giles, D. E. (1999). *Where's the learning in service-learning?* San Francisco, CA: Jossey-Bass.

Freire, P. (2000). *Pedagogy of the oppressed* (20th anniversary ed.). New York, NY: Continuum.

Furco, A. (1999). *Self-assessment rubric for the institutionalization of service-learning in higher education.* Berkeley, CA: Service-Learning Research and Development Center, University of California, Berkeley.

Gelmon, S. B., Holland, B. A., Driscoll, A., Spring, A., & Kerrigan, S. (2001). *Assessing service-learning and civic engagement: Principles and techniques.* Providence, RI: Campus Compact.

Gent, P. J. (2007). Strange bedfellows: No Child Left Behind and service-learning. *Michigan Journal of Community Service Learning, 13*(2), 65–74.

Goleman, D. (1995). *Emotional intelligence.* New York, NY: Bantam Books.

Goleman, D. (2004, January). What makes a leader? *Harvard Business Review*, 4–12.

Heldman, C. (2011). Solidarity, not charity: Issues of privilege in service-learning. In C. M. Cress & D. M. Donahue (Eds.), *Democratic dilemmas of teaching service-learning: Curricular strategies for success* (pp. 33–42). Sterling, VA: Stylus.

Holloran, P., & Carson, C. (Eds.). (2000). *A knock at midnight: Inspiration from the great sermons of Reverend Martin Luther King, Jr.* New York, NY: Warner Books.

Jacoby, B. (2003). *Building partnerships for service-learning.* San Francisco, CA: Jossey-Bass.

Kawashima-Ginsberg, K., Lim, C., & Levine, P. (2012). *Civic health and unemployment II: The case builds.* Washington, DC: National Conference on Citizenship.

Keen, C., & Hall, K. (2009). Engaging with difference matters: Longitudinal student outcomes of co-curricular service-learning programs. *Journal of Higher Education, 80*(1), 59–79.

Lupton, R. D. (2012). *Toxic charity: How churches and charities hurt those they help (and how to reverse it).* New York, NY: HarperOne.

Lutkehaus, N. C. (2008). *Margaret Mead: The making of an American icon.* Princeton, NJ: Princeton University Press.

Mitchell, T. D. (2008). Traditional vs. critical service-learning: Engaging the literature to differentiate two models. *Michigan Journal of Community Service-Learning, 14*(2), 50–65.

National Conference on Citizenship. (2011). *Civic health and unemployment: Can engagement strengthen the economy?* Washington, DC: Author.

National Task Force on Civic Learning and Democratic Engagement. (2012). *A crucible moment: College learning and democracy's future.* Washington, DC: Association of American Colleges and Universities. Retrieved from www.aacu.org/civic_learning/crucible

O'Meara, K. A., & Rice, R. E. (Eds.). (2005). *Faculty priorities reconsidered: Encouraging multiple forms of scholarship.* San Francisco, CA: Jossey-Bass.

Perry, W. G. (1970). *Forms of intellectual and ethical development in the college years: A scheme.* New York, NY: Holt, Rinehart, and Winston.

Plaut, J., Cress, C., Ikeda, E., & McGinley, P. (2013). *Partnering in tough times: Service-learning for economic vitality.* Palo Alto, CA: California Campus Compact.

Pompa, L. (2002). Service-learning as crucible: Reflections on immersion, context, power, and transformation. *Michigan Journal of Community Service Learning, 9*(1), 67–76.

Rabbit-duck illusion. Retrieved August 1, 2014, from http://upload.wikimedia.org/wikipedia/commons/1/13/PSM_V54_D328_Optical_illusion_of_a_duck_or_a_rabbit_head.png

Reitenauer, V. L., Cress, C. M., & Bennett, J. (2013). Creating cultural connections: Navigating difference, investigating power, unpacking privilege. In C. M. Cress, P. J. Collier, & V. L. Reitenauer (Eds.), *Learning through serving: A student guidebook for service-learning and civic engagement across academic disciplines and cultural communities* (pp. 77–91). Sterling, VA: Stylus.

Rhoads, R. A. (1998). Critical multiculturalism and service learning. In R. A. Rhoads & J. P. F. Howard (Eds.), *Academic service learning: A pedagogy of action and reflection* (pp. 39–46). San Francisco, CA: Jossey-Bass.

Rice, K., & Pollack, S. (2000). Developing a critical pedagogy of service learning: Preparing self-reflective, culturally aware, and responsive community participants. In C. R. O'Grady (Ed.), *Integrating service learning and multicultural education in colleges and universities* (pp. 115–134). Mahwah, NJ: Lawrence Erlbaum.

Rosenberger, C. (2000). Beyond empathy: Developing critical consciousness through service learning. In C. R. O'Grady (Ed.), *Integrating service learning and multicultural education in colleges and universities* (pp. 23–43). Mahwah, NJ: Lawrence Erlbaum.

Sandy, M., & Holland, B. (2006). Different worlds and common ground: Community partner perspectives on campus–community partnerships. *Michigan Journal of Community Service Learning, 13*(1), 30–43.

Torres, J. (2000). *Benchmarks for campus/community partnerships.* Boston, MA: Campus Compact.

Vogelgesang, L. (2004). Diversity work and service-learning: Understanding campus dynamics. *Michigan Journal of Community Service Learning, 10*(2), 34–43.

Vygotsky, L. (1978). *Mind in society: The development of higher psychological processes.* Cam-
bridge, MA: Harvard University Press.

Wiewel, W. (2010). Building 21st century universities for Oregon. *Oregonian,* p. B8.

Wilber, K. (1999). *The marriage of sense and soul: Integrating science and religion.* New York,
NY: Random House.

Resources for Co-Educators in Service-Learning

Organizations

These organizations have resources for service-learning practitioners in academia and in the community.

Association of American Colleges and Universities
www.aacu.org/ (see especially *civic learning* and *global learning* tabs)

Association of Americans for Civic Responsibility
www.aacri.org/index.aspx

Campus Compact (many U.S. states also have a Campus Compact chapter office with more local resources and information)
www.compact.org

Carnegie Foundation
www.carnegiefoundation.org

Center for Civic Education
www.civiced.org

Center for Civic Reflection
www.civicreflection.org

CIRCLE (Center for Information and Research on Civic Learning and Engagement)
http://civicyouth.org

Civic Practices Network
www.cpn.org

Community-Campus Partnerships for Health
http://ccph.memberclicks.net/

Community Service Partners, Inc.
www.communityservicepartners.org

Corporation for National and Community Service (AmeriCorps and others)
www.nationalservice.gov

Hands On Network
www.handsonnetwork.org

Idealist
www.idealist.org

International Association for Research on Service-Learning and Community Engagement (IARSLCE)
www.researchslce.org

Kettering Foundation
www.kettering.org

National Service-Learning Partnership
www.service-learningpartnership.org

National Youth Leadership Council
www.nylc.org

Volunteers of America, Oregon
www.voaor.org

Handbooks and Guides

Many colleges and universities have resources for community partners available on their websites. These sites often include links to documents or forms used by that institution, such as time logs, community partner agreements, and photo release forms. Check your local campus partner's website or see these examples.

California State University Channel Islands
www.csuci.edu/servicelearning/communitypartners.htm

Fordham University
http://legacy.fordham.edu/mission/mission_and_ministry/dorothy_day_center_f/service_learning_pro/for_community_partne_74468.asp

Gettysburg College
www.gettysburg.edu/about/offices/college_life/cps/community

Marquette University
www.marquette.edu/servicelearning/current_community_partner_resources.shtml

Owens Community College
www.owens.edu/service/community.html
Portland State University
http://www.pdx.edu/elp/service-learning

University of Tennessee, Knoxville
http://servicelearning.utk.edu/community-partner-resources

Virginia Commonwealth University
http://www.community.vcu.edu/resources--toolkit/toolkit/

Literature

Selected Books and Journals

There is a growing body of research and writing devoted to campus-community partnerships. The following resources are not comprehensive but provide an indication of the kinds of readings available to further your own knowledge.

Cress, C. M., Collier, P. J., & Reitenauer, V. L. (2013). *Learning through serving: A student guidebook for service-learning across academic disciplines and cultural communities* (2nd ed.). Sterling, VA: Stylus.

Cress, C. M., & Donahue, D. A. (2011). *Democratic dilemmas of teaching service-learning: Curricular strategies for success.* Sterling, VA: Stylus.

Gelmon, S., Holland, B., Driscoll, A., Spring, A., & Kerrigan, S. (2001). *Assessing service-learning and civic engagement: Principles and techniques.* Providence, RI: Campus Compact.

Harter, L., Hamel-Lambert, J., & Millesen, J. (Eds.). (2010). *Participatory partnerships for social action and research.* Dubuque, IA: Kendall Hunt.

Jacoby, B. (2003). *Building partnerships for service-learning.* San Francisco, CA: Jossey-Bass.

Stoecker, R., & Tryon, E. (Eds.). (2009). *The unheard voices: Community organizations and service-learning.* Philadelphia, PA: Temple University Press.

University of North Carolina at Greensboro and North Carolina Campus Compact. *Partnerships: A journal of service-learning and civic engagement.* Retrieved from http://libjournal.uncg.edu/index.php/prt

Selected Chapters and Articles

Avila, M. (with Knoerr, A., Orlando, N., & Castillo, C.). (2010). Community organizing practices in academia: A model and stories of partnerships. *Journal of Higher Education Outreach and Engagement, 14*(2), 37–63.

Bushouse, B. K. (2005). Community nonprofit organizations and service-learning: Resource constraints to building partnerships with universities. *Michigan Journal of Community Service Learning, 12*(1), 32–40.

Carmichael Strong, E., Green, P. M., Meyer, M., & Post, M. A. (2009). Future directions in campus-community partnerships. In J. Strait & M. Lima (Eds.), *The future of service-learning: New solutions for sustaining and improving practice* (pp. 9–32). Sterling, VA: Stylus.

Cress, C. M., Burack, C., Giles, D. E., Jr., Elkins, J., & Stevens, M. C. (2010). *A promising connection: Increasing college access and success through civic engagement*. Boston, MA: Campus Compact.

D'Arlach, L., Sanchez, B., & Feuer, R. (2009). Voices from the community: A case for reciprocity in service-learning. *Michigan Journal of Community Service Learning, 16*(1), 5–16. Retrieved from http://quod.lib.umich.edu/m/mjcsl/

Dorado, S., & Giles, D. (2004). Service-learning partnerships: Paths of engagement. *Michigan Journal of Community Service Learning, 11*(1), 25–37. Retrieved from http://quod.lib.umich.edu/m/mjcsl/

Kecskes, K. (2006). Behind the rhetoric: Applying a cultural theory lens to campus-community partnership development. *Michigan Journal for Community Service Learning, 12*(2), 5–14. Retrieved from http://quod.lib.umich.edu/m/mjcsl/

Miron, D., & Moely, B. E. (2006). Community agency voice and benefit in service-learning. *Michigan Journal of Community Service-Learning, 12*(2), 27–37.

Plaut, J., Cress, C. M., Ikeda, E., & McGinley, P. (2013). *Partnering in tough times: Service-learning for economic vitality*. Palo Alto, CA: California Campus Compact.

Sandy, M., & Holland, B. (2006). Different worlds and common ground: Community partner perspectives on campus-community partnerships. *Michigan Journal of Community Service Learning, 13*(1), 30–43. Retrieved from http://quod.lib.umich.edu/m/mjcsl/

Strand, K., Marullo, S., Cutforth, N., Stoecker, R., & Donohue, P. (2003). Principles of best practice for community-based research. *Michigan Journal of Community Service Learning, 9*(3), 5–15. Retrieved from http://quod.lib.umich.edu/m/mjcsl/

Worrall, L. (2007). Asking the community: A case study of community partner perspectives. *Michigan Journal of Community Service Learning, 14*(1), 5–17. Retrieved from http://quod.lib.umich.edu/m/mjcsl/

This edition presents four new chapters on Mentoring, Leadership, Becoming a Change Agent, and Short-Term Immersive and Global Service-Learning experiences. The authors have also revised the original chapters to more fully address issues of social justice, privilege/power, diversity, intercultural communication, and technology; have added more disciplinary examples; incorporated additional academic content for understanding service-learning issues (e.g., attribution theory); and cover issues related to students with disabilities, and international students.

Sty/us

22883 Quicksilver Drive
Sterling, VA 20166-2102

Subscribe to our e-mail alerts: www.Styluspub.com

Learning Through Serving

A Student Guidebook for Service-Learning and Civic Engagement Across Academic Disciplines and Cultural Communities

Second Edition

Christine M. Cress, Peter J. Collier, and Vicki L. Reitenauer

Reviews of the first edition

"[This] is a self-directed guide for college students engaged in service-learning. The purpose of the book is to walk the reader through elements of learning and serving by focusing on how students can 'best provide meaningful service to a community agency or organization while simultaneously gaining new skills, knowledge, and understanding as an integrated aspect of the [student's] academic program.' [The authors] bring their expertise to the pages of this helpful and practical guide for college students engaged in service-learning. Intended as a textbook, this work reads like a conversation between the authors and the college student learner. The publication is student-friendly, comprehensive, easy to follow, and full of helpful activities."

—*Journal of College Student Development*

"Finally, a companion reader for students in service-learning courses! It is filled with meaningful exercises to help students make sense of their service experience and relate it to the course content. This is an important contribution to the field of service learning and faculty should utilize this book to help students understand and make the most of their service-learning experience."

—*Elaine K. Ikeda*, *Executive Director, California Campus Compact*

This substantially expanded new edition of this widely used and acclaimed text maintains the objectives and tenets of the first. It is designed to help students understand and reflect on their community service experiences both as individuals and as citizens of communities in need of their compassionate expertise. It is designed to assist faculty in facilitating student development of compassionate expertise through the context of service in applying disciplinary knowledge to community issues and challenges. In sum, the book is about how to make academic sense of civic service in preparing for roles as future citizen leaders.

(continued)